ARTPRENEUR

THE STEP-BY-STEP GUIDE TO MAKING A SUSTAINABLE LIVING FROM YOUR
CREATIVITY

MIRIAM SCHULMAN

HarperCollins
LEADERSHIP

An Imprint of HarperCollins

Published by HarperCollins Leadership,
an imprint of HarperCollins Focus LLC.

Book design by Aubrey Khan, Neuwirth & Associates, Inc.

Stethoscope icon by Rokhman Kharis from Noun Project
Pill container icon by mitochondrial from Noun Project

ISBN 978-1-4002-3515-5 (eBook)
ISBN 978-1-4002-3514-8 (TP)

Library of Congress Cataloging-in-Publication Data
Library of Congress Cataloging-in-Publication
application has been submitted.

Printed in the United States of America
23 24 25 26 27 LSC 10 9 8 7 6 5 4 3 2 1

"This is the book artists need to debunk all the myths keeping them stuck. If you are looking for success in your career, Miriam has written an excellent blueprint to follow." **—MARIA BRITO,** bestselling author of *How Creativity Rules the World*

"Attention all artists, writers, and musicians! This is one of the most actionable books that will turn your creative side hustle into a legit business. You need this!" **—AMY PORTERFIELD,** podcast host and author of *Two Weeks Notice*

"The ultimate blueprint for creatives to get seen, heard, and PAID well." **—JENNIFER KEM,** CEO of Master Brand Institute

"Miriam gives the proverbial marketing color swatch so that we can have more well-fed and happy artists!" **—TODD HERMAN,** author of *The Alter Ego Effect*

"Finally, there is a creative call to arms for the aspiring professional artist! This book shows that talent and money can coexist." **—JEANNE OLIVER,** creator of Creatively Made Business

"Miriam Schulman gives you a trustworthy roadmap to running your creative empire!" **—JENNIFER DASAL,** author of *ArtCurious*

"Artists need to know: *Artpreneur* is money in the bank." **—SUSIE MOORE,** bestselling author of *Let It Be Easy*

"Miriam will show you how to turn your passion into a viable, successful career you can pursue with confidence. She knows how—she's done it!" **—DANNY GREGORY,** CEO of Sketchbook Skool

"Most artists grow up being told 'you can't make money doing that.' *Artpreneur* challenges that belief and fuels artists' ability to earn a real living."
—**ANDREA OWEN,**
author of *Make Some Noise*

"*Artpreneur* will give you everything you need to make your art career profitable, successful, and personally rewarding." —**JO PACKHAM,**
editor in chief of the *Women Create* magazine series

"Simple, actionable, and inspiring—and it leads creatives straight to the bank." —**TRACY OTSUKA,**
host of the *ADHD for Smart Ass Women* podcast

"If you're ready to take charge of your art life, this is the book for you!"
—**ERIC MAISEL,**
author of *Coaching the Artist Within*

"With warmth and chutzpah, Miriam teaches artists how to market and (gasp!) sell." —**GIGI ROSENBERG,**
author of *The Artist's Guide to Grant Writing*

"*Artpreneur* is the ultimate guide to building a lucrative career as an artist!" —**SELENA SOO,**
creator of Impacting Millions

"All creative people can use *Artpreneur* to put their work into the world, get it seen, and get paid for it without any of the guilt."
—**MICHAEL F. SCHEIN,**
author of *The Hype Handbook*

"Whether you're struggling to make consistent sales or dreaming of turning your art into a full-time living, *Artpreneur* provides the inspiration and practical steps you need." —**MATTHEW POLLARD,**
bestselling author of *The Introvert's Edge*

"If you are hesitant to make the leap to the artist's life, be forewarned. Schulman will convince you that you can't afford to wait any longer."
—**ALYSON STANFIELD,**
author of *I'd Rather Be in the Studio!*

"*Artpreneur* is the artist handbook I wish I had when I started out."
—**ABBEY SY,**
artist and author of *The Art of the Travel Journal*

CONTENTS

+ + + + + + + +

"EVERY TIME YOU STATE
WHAT YOU WANT OR
BELIEVE, YOU'RE THE FIRST
TO HEAR IT. IT'S A MESSAGE
TO BOTH YOU AND OTHERS
ABOUT WHAT YOU THINK IS
POSSIBLE."

—OPRAH WINFREY

CHOOSE TO BELIEVE

IN THE HOT ATLANTA CLASSROOM, the backs of my thighs stuck to my wooden desk chair. I was pulling a stray thread from my hem when my fourth-grade teacher, Mrs. McNair, held up a piece of green felt over her white frothy hair and drawled in a thick southern accent, "Does anyone know what this is?"

My hand shot up as I blurted out. "An eighth!"

Mrs. McNair peered at me over the edge of her half-moon spectacles and pressed her thin lips together as the other kids sniggered. Apparently, the correct answer was "a fraction." Annoyed, I slumped back in my chair and resumed picking at the hem. As the new girl at school, I hadn't quite caught on that it was time to swap dresses for denim shorts, but I knew an eighth when I saw it—the same shape as a perfectly sized piece of pie.

Later that day, she pulled me aside. At first, I thought I was in trouble for calling out in class, but instead she explained that every class in the elementary school designed a jack-o'-lantern for Halloween. My fraction outburst had demonstrated a good understanding of shapes and proportions, so she wanted me to be the "class artist" and design our pumpkin.

This marked the first time in my life that I had been called an artist, or had even thought of myself that way. Like Harry Potter being named a wizard for the first time, "artist" was a label that caught me off guard, yet it made perfect sense. This new identity explained my unique ability to look at an ordinary piece of felt and see something others could not, and from that moment on I began to see myself differently. The simple truth was, my teacher declared that I was an artist, and I chose to believe her. Eventually, this belief drove me to answer the call. Perhaps you've felt that call as well. To declare oneself an artist isn't easy, but believing in yourself is a critical part of the belief triad for selling your art. (We'll get to that in chapter 3.)

ANSWER THE CALL

If you've felt that call and are struggling to sell your own art, I get it. There are countless business courses to take, gurus to follow, tech tools to choose from, and numerous conflicting voices about what you "really need" to be successful. And there's a lot of bad advice out there, which is why I want to help you cut through that noise.

There has never been a better time to turn your creative ideas into a successful business. The art world gatekeepers no longer decide what is "worthy"; the internet has leveled the playing field. Today, anyone with a laptop and a dream can make a sustainable living from their creativity. So why are so many artists still struggling? Many artists just lack a solid foundation in how to market and sell or are so overwhelmed with information that they're doubting their next moves. Many artists are both confused and overwhelmed, with too much conflicting advice and no idea about where to start.

In this book, we refer to anyone who practices any of the creative arts, such as a filmmaker, novelist, poet, sculptor—whether it's done professionally or not—as an artist. Regardless of your talent, you were an artist the moment you created your first finger painting or twirled in the backyard to your own happy, made-up song. There's no magic fairy (or fourth-grade teacher) who deems anyone an artist. You get to decide to wear that crown. You can be an artist and create just for fun, but if you want to make a thriving business out of it and become a true artpreneur, you'll need to develop the mindset and learn the business skills that entrepreneurship requires. In this book you'll get both.

Many of my examples will come from the world of visual art, the one with which I'm most familiar. However, the advice here is derived from the business world. The elements of business success are for all entrepreneurs and all *artpreneurs*, no matter what kind of art you create.

THE ELEMENTS OF BUSINESS SUCCESS

In building a sustainable business, the five core elements of your business that will drive your success are: production, pricing, prospecting, promotion, and productivity. Together, these elements comprise what I call the Passion-to-Profit framework, which forms the foundation of all successful businesses. Many artists struggle as artpreneurs because they've got a problem in one or more of these areas, and, worse yet, they often misidentify the problem! We'll dive deeper into each area in chapter 5 and uncover common mistakes that lead to art-marketing malpractice. In addition, chapters 6 through 11 will go deeper into each element, with two chapters dedicated to helping you learn how to actually sell your art.

Now, what if I told you that the biggest factor impacting your ability to build your business is confidence? Would you believe me? Deep down, I bet you know that if you had more confidence, it would unlock all kinds of opportunities for you. Confidence runs along a spectrum, which I call the *belief scale*. And where you land on the belief scale will either enhance or impair your ability to price, prospect, promote, and continue to produce your art. Throughout the book you'll be guided through "thought work" exercises that will help you identify when you're having thought distortions and replace limiting beliefs with empowering artpreneur thinking.

Your mindset controls everything, and when you have positive thoughts, they generate the emotions you need to act. With a positive mindset you can take the bravest actions—the ones that make the most difference. When you believe in possibility, those positive thoughts motivate you. Conversely, when you lack belief, you'll feel discouraged, which dampens your motivation and inhibits action. Your thoughts drive how you see the world, how you perceive others, your choices, and, ultimately, your actions, which determine your results. Creating an abundance mindset is the sixth element you need to succeed; this book will help bolster your mindset and confidence so that you will. Confidence building is baked into this book to kick the starving-artist mentality to the curb. In chapter 7, you'll even get fourteen "abundant artist lessons" when it comes to pricing your art.

LIMITING BELIEFS

Many artists have one or more self-sabotaging thoughts. I must confess, at one time or another I didn't believe I could make a living as an artist (which is why I never went to art school). Saddled with student loans, I took the practical route and headed for Wall Street. Although I loved the income, I felt disconnected from my life purpose. After 9/11, I knew I couldn't remain in the corporate world. Yet at the time I didn't believe I could make a full-time living from my art either. That self-defeating thought held me back for many years.

Any thoughts that inhibit you from taking positive actions are known as "limiting beliefs." Sometimes we're even aware that these unwelcome thoughts aren't true, but often we perceive limiting beliefs as facts. For example, you may be thinking, "I'm not good enough," or "No one wants to pay high prices for art," and to you this feels like fact. However, this exaggerated, all-or-nothing way of perceiving a situation is a thought *distortion*. In many thought distortions, a seed of truth masks the limiting belief underlying it.

So, what's the difference between a limiting belief and a thought distortion? The late psychologist Dr. Aaron Beck, who founded the principles of cognitive behavioral therapy (CBT), recognized that people have core beliefs that are a result of our upbringing, cultural and social conditioning, and life experiences. All of us have a belief system that stems from our core values; however, we also have what Dr. Beck called "self-defeating beliefs" that get triggered. Throughout this book, we'll refer to self-defeating beliefs with the more common term "limiting beliefs." Moreover, Dr. Beck's work demonstrated that people have what he called "cognitive distortions." I prefer the term "thought distortion." When we have a distorted view of reality, we may think thoughts that are overgeneralized or black and white. Since limiting beliefs are based on your belief system, you can't prove them to be true or false. For example, you might have a limiting belief that people shouldn't have to pay high prices for art, or the earlier example, "I'm not good enough." These statements can't be proven true or false because they're opinions. On the other hand, a thought distortion might take the form of "people won't pay high prices for art." Since that's a belief that *can* be proven true or false, it's easier to question it. Psychiatrist and CBT pioneer Dr. David Burns writes on his blog, "When you challenge and defeat a distorted thought, you feel better in the here and now. When you challenge and change a SDB [limiting belief], you change your value system at a deep level."[1]

The thought work throughout this book will poke holes into many of your established beliefs, which will create a change in your thinking. Your results will reflect any limitations you believe; therefore, fixing even *one* thought distortion will unlock all kinds of success for you. Throughout this book, I'll help you recognize your thought distortions and limiting beliefs by calling them out and suggesting thoughts that will be more helpful.

MEET FAYE, an artist from Baltimore who started working with me during the coronavirus pandemic in 2020. While she was still working full-time as an event planner, she was satisfied with sporadic sales of her art that she did on the side. But once she was furloughed, and newly divorced, Faye was determined to turn her art into a full-time living. She had been selling her figurative paintings for under $50 each because she believed that "cheaper is easier to sell." However, in all of 2019, her art sales had totaled a paltry $300.

I told Faye that the first thing she needed to do was raise prices on her art and create larger works that would command even higher price points. Frowning, Faye admitted, "I'm afraid of what people will think." She proceeded to list all the reasons why this strategy wouldn't work for her. When she noticed my raised eyebrows, she stopped talking.

Cue my New York brand of tough love (with an unapologetic New York accent): "If you want a small hobby, keep painting small and asking for small prices. If you want a big art career that can support you and your children, you'll need to dream big and paint big—with big price tags to match."

For all women, the pressure to stay small is tough conditioning to overcome. Proof of this is everywhere, from distorted Barbie dolls to the billion-dollar weight-loss industry constantly hammering women with messages to be thinner (i.e., smaller). And according to ABC News, most fashion models that we admire meet the criteria for anorexia.[2] On the other hand, boys are delivered the opposite narrative. The typical male Disney character is a muscular brute, whereas the Disney princess is a fragile waif. (Of course, body dysmorphia is a rising problem for boys as well.)[3] These messages of size affect more than just our waistlines. Society is essentially telling women to take up as little space as possible, a disempowering message on all levels. This is also quite evident on public transport, where men routinely splay their legs without regard for other passengers and women are expected to sit with legs glued together or crossed to take up as little space as possible.

For women of color like Faye, the pressure to stay quiet and play small persists throughout their lives. Diversity content specialist A. Rochaun Meadows-Fernandez writes, "The early lessons we teach Black children suggest that they should take up as little space as possible if they want to survive in the world. But that safety comes at a cost. It locks us into a life of mediocracy and tells us the price of following our dreams is too high."[4]

Within a few months of our working together, Faye learned to stop thinking of her business as "little" and dropped the starving-artist mentality. She began painting larger and charging more, asking $1,400 and up for her art.

Moreover, she found that higher-priced art was actually *easier* to sell. This breakthrough in thinking enabled her to start enjoying five-figure months, and she now regularly sells out 90 percent of her collections. As a result, she's on her way to a sustainable living as a true artpreneur. Just like Faye, I'll help you have your own breakthrough in thinking about how to price your art, no matter what kind of art you create.

THINK LIKE AN ARTPRENEUR

When I first began selling my art, I felt overwhelmed and discouraged by the band of bro-marketers pushing the hustle culture, which didn't speak to the realities of my world. Like many women, I'd been told that I'm "too loud"—but part of being an artist is owning your artistic voice with no apologies. I've also been told I'm too Jewish, too ethnic, and asked to tone down my cultural references, but no one hears you when you've got your volume turned down to a whisper. I wish I had a guide to hold my hand and show me what works and what doesn't—and, most importantly, to teach me to chip away at the prevalent and damaging stories that affect women artists: the myth of the starving artist, the cult of the male genius, and the lie that women must choose between motherhood and success. This book is that guide. And although I identify and empathize with the realities women face, this is a handbook that will help *all* emerging artists, no matter your gender. You'll learn how to think like a successful artist, an artpreneur, as we work together to dismantle the self-sabotaging beliefs that hinder your momentum and profits. Plus, you'll learn how to apply to your own business the traditional sales and marketing techniques within my Passion-to-Profit framework.

HOW I MADE IT AS AN ARTPRENEUR

In high school, I filled my notebooks with pen-and-ink sketches of teachers, caricatures of classmates, and hand lettering. (Font study began in the third grade, when I rebelled against the blue-lined paper.) In college, I jeopardized my financial-aid package when I formally switched my major from engineering to art history. While working on Wall Street, I continued to incorporate art in my life by taking workshops in my spare time with renowned watercolor artists. Of course, my earliest attempts at watercolor were dreadful, but to be good at anything, you must be willing to be bad at first. I spent countless hours developing the techniques I use today. And finally, after witnessing the devastation that occurred on 9/11, I took that as a sign from the universe and answered the call to become an artist.

When I quit my finance job over twenty years ago, I had my hands full with a newborn and a toddler. Even so, I kept painting on the side during naptime. To make ends meet, I taught Pilates, and the gym introduced me to marketing techniques that they used for selling personal training packages. It was then that I had my "aha" moment and realized that these time-tested methods could be used to sell *anything*, including art.

Many of my strategies for selling art are so basic that they're laughable, and yet they work. (Spoiler alert: Handing out business cards is *not* one of them!) When I started my art business, we didn't have social media, which is why most of my marketing still relies on time-tested principles. Yes, social media has its place, but we artists spend enough time on our phones, and our creative energy is best saved for creating beautiful art rather than more content for the Zuckerverse. Social media is a fickle friend and constantly changing. You'll learn in these pages how to tap into the power of using social media for direct messaging; however, I see too many artists (and entrepreneurs in general) spending more time than is necessary on social media to build their businesses. Research from Agency Analytics shows that email marketing is more effective than social media in nearly every category. For example, the average rate of someone clicking on one of your emails is 2.5 percent, whereas on Facebook the average click-through rate is a paltry .07 percent. And when it comes to profit, you can expect to earn $38 for every dollar invested in email marketing whereas the return on investment on Facebook is only 28 cents.[5]

This book focuses on traditional list-building over social media, not because it's "old-fashioned" but because it's what works the best and will make you the most money as an artist. Marie Forleo, who teaches thousands of people to build online businesses, proclaims, "I do think that people are spending less time on social or recognizing some of those negative impacts ... there's going to be a move away from social even more in the upcoming years. I think it's critical that people up their ability and understanding of email marketing and how to make it effective."[6] In other words, the future of marketing is not social media.

The old-school marketing methods I applied worked so well that within a year I had a waitlist for portraits and was earning over $24,000 a year from my art. In the second year, I doubled my art income. (Goodbye, sweaty gym—except for going there as a *client*.) A few years after that, I had built a sustainable art business all outside the traditional gallery system, and *without paid advertising*. Then, in 2012, an Etsy customer asked me if I offered online art classes. Back then I was unfamiliar with digital courses, but I was intrigued and wanted to figure out how to do it. Taking a leap of faith, I created The Inspiration Place, a platform for online learning.

I naively imagined that all I had to do was publish a few posts about my new class on social media—but all I got from those first attempts was crickets. Meanwhile, I saw other artists offering online classes, and they made it look so *easy*. After building an email list, I finally figured out how to connect with students in the virtual world. Armed with these additional marketing techniques, I implemented better strategies, which I used to sell my classes *and* my art. Popularity in my online classes soared, pushing my income over the six-figure mark. I felt like I had so much to share about how I built my business over the last twenty years that I created *The Inspiration Place* podcast to give a voice to my story. After dozens of episodes on mindset, marketing, building your email list, attracting high-end commissions, and more, people begged me for a way to get more personalized help. This is why I developed the Artist Incubator Coaching Program to work with artists to go beyond the technique and grow thriving art businesses—so that they can have the time and freedom to create art and do what they love.[7] These methods work well for the artists I've coached over the years (and you'll meet some of them in these pages). If you apply what you learn here, these techniques will also work for you.

NOW IT'S YOUR TURN

You picked up this book for a reason. Have you heard those creative whispers? There's an artist in each of us wanting to break free. Your muse is tired of staying quiet and waiting for you to feel ready, take the next step, or dream bigger. You are enough. You are more than capable. And I want you to have the same confidence in running your business as you have in your incredible talent. To be successful, you must first get comfortable with owning your desire to want more wealth and visibility. Moreover, you need to see yourself as priceless before you can put a price tag on anything you create. I urge you to gamble on yourself and not give up on your dreams. Don't worry. In these pages, you'll find all the steps you need to evolve into that next version of yourself.

WHAT ARTPRENEURS NEED TO BELIEVE

- There's never been a better time to turn your creative ideas into a successful business.
- When it comes to building a sustainable business, five elements will be responsible for your success as an artpreneur: production, pricing, prospecting, promotion, and productivity.
- Fixing even one limiting belief will unlock all kinds of success for you.
- Artists spend enough time on their phones, and their creativity should be saved for creating beautiful art rather than content for the Zuckerverse.

MARCHING ORDERS

- Declare your identity as an artist. Tell everyone you meet that you're an artist, writer, musician, poet, playwright, or whatever form of artist moniker suits you.
- Do this from a place of sharing, service, and connection—without trying to sell them anything! Sharing your artistic identity is connection; hiding your identity is not.
- Practice showing up in the world as an artist. Repeatedly telling everyone that you're an artist is how you begin to rewrite your story. This is key for two reasons: it will strengthen belief in your identity, and at the same time you'll develop the skill of articulating what you do and why. These are essential skills for all artpreneurs.

"REMEMBER THAT YOU MUST BUILD YOUR LIFE AS IF IT WERE A WORK OF ART."

—RABBI ABRAHAM JOSHUA HESCHEL

BREAK FREE OF THE GOLDEN HANDCUFFS

WHEN I TELL PEOPLE THAT I used to work in finance, they all say the same thing: "You must've *hated* that." They can't reconcile the hippy-dippy artist they see now with the image of a suited-up banker. But before I became a full-time artpreneur, I had a whole other life, and I understand how it feels to be tied to a job. Though I wanted to be an artist, my Jewish mother feared I'd never make any money—and I believed her. She had expected me to become a doctor, a doctor's wife, or a disappointment.

When I graduated, I was staring down a mountain of student debt. I figured if the point was to make as much money as possible, I might as well follow my fractions talent to a high-paying job on Wall Street. The immediate relief of an over-the-top salary gave me the economic freedom I'd always deemed for *other* people. For the first time in my life, I could walk into an Ann Taylor store and pay full price. But my high-paying job came with a high price tag as well; and over time I began to resent the golden handcuffs.

The more money I made, the harder it was to imagine leaving. I felt safe in that cave with my cushy salary and benefits, and I feared the tigers on the outside. I had grown up in a single-parent household and I worried that if I gave up this job, I'd be repeating the poverty of my childhood. I was earning more than my husband, and we planned to start a family in a few years. We wanted our children to have a better life than we did. I thought staying put kept me safe, but in reality it left me vulnerable to dangers I'd never imagined would be inside the cave.

I hear from so many creatives who long to become full-time artists but are afraid to escape their safe job. If that's you, know that I see you and that I've been there too. If you've ever put up with an abusive boss, or a job out of alignment with your life purpose, you might see yourself in my story but with different details. Here's how I made the leap from the corporate life to full-time artpreneurship.

LIAR'S POKER

When I accepted the $65,000 job offer from Salomon Brothers in 1992, my manager handed me a dog-eared copy of Michael Lewis's *Liar's Poker* as if it were the employee handbook. This bestselling book chronicled Lewis's years at Salomon, then one of the five largest investment banks in the world and the most profitable on Wall Street.[1] While Lewis joined the other (mostly White) male traders on the forty-second floor of 7 World Trade Center, I landed an analyst job for the back office a few stories below.

My work involved writing computer programs that calculated the value of derivatives. This work made the firm millions and fueled those male traders' high-flying lifestyles. (Derivatives also have the potential to lose billions, bankrupt local governments,[2] and bring entire financial systems to their knees.) Though their trades weren't possible without our complex computer programs, our group never gained access to the C-suite or the trading floor. As a financial analyst, I was well paid—just not the heady numbers of the mostly White male trading elite. To keep us happy, management rewarded us with fancy, wine-soaked dinners, imported cigars (if we wanted them), and box seats at exclusive sporting events, like the World Cup. However, such gifts groomed us to tolerate increasing levels of abuse.

In the opening chapter of *Liar's Poker*, Lewis describes the popular card game played for high stakes by the top traders. You might have played this game as a child under the name "I Doubt It"—where success depends on your ability to deceive your opponents about the cards you really hold in your hands. In other words, good liars make great players. Lewis describes how the traders kept a running tab of the *thousands* of dollars they nonchalantly bet each day. To illustrate the carelessness with which these men played with their money, Lewis narrates how John Gutfreund, the cigar-chomping CEO and "King of Wall Street,"[3] bet John Meriwether, the head of the bond-trading desk, a million dollars on a hand of Liar's Poker. Surely the CEO was bluffing, but if Meriwether won, he would embarrass his boss—a no-win situation. In the end, Meriwether negotiated his way out of it by upping the ante to ten million.

I didn't believe a word of it.

To get the lowdown, I asked Jason,[4] an analyst who had been working there for some time. "The first part of the story, the million-dollar bet—that happened," he said as he reached into his pocket. He pulled out an engraved silver cigar cutter and gave it an ominous snap. With a wink, he slowly slid his index finger into the round opening and whispered into my hair, "The counteroffer was for a *finger*."

I'll never know whether either version of that wild Liar's Poker bet was true, but I did learn that the men I worked for had a fluid relationship with the truth. I have a bitter remembrance of that fluidity from one cold day in the corporate cafeteria. I was about to ask my friend Victoria if she wanted to sneak in a quick walk after lunch, when the power suddenly went out. Management told us it was a ConEd (energy supply company) failure. We believed them—even though ambulances and fire trucks were already circling our building.

Our building's backup generator brought the lights back on, but the elevators were completely out of commission. Mind you, this was 1993, with no smartphones to give us instant access to helpful information. Consequently, Victoria and I headed for the stairs and climbed up thirty-seven floors to return to our desks.

From the windows of our building, 7 World Trade Center, we saw the chilling sight of the North Tower. Smoke poured out of broken windows, and helicopters circled the skies. This was no ConEd failure. While we were at lunch, a bomb had exploded in the parking garage beneath the complex, knocking a wide hole through four levels of concrete and sending black smoke through the Twin Towers.[5] As in our building, the power in the Twin Towers went out immediately. With no electricity or running elevators, thousands of people were trapped inside and forced to evacuate through the smoke-filled staircases in complete darkness. People trapped in the building smashed windows with their computers in a futile effort to clear the air.

Though that 1993 bombing of the World Trade Center has of course been overshadowed by 9/11, it was frightening to witness in person. And what were my coworkers (who by then knew the truth) doing when I arrived on that floor? Were they evacuating the building? Nope. Were they calling their loved ones? No. Since our backup generators kept the computers humming, my coworkers and bosses remained glued to their desks—working. The culture of Wall Street is that you work no matter what, and the culture of *Liar's Poker* is that you don't give in to your emotions. Even during a terrorist attack in the building adjacent to ours, we were expected to do our jobs for the rest of the day. I slipped out the side door, sprinted down thirty-seven flights of stairs, and contacted my husband as soon as I could.

NOT READY YET

I wish I could tell you I made my decision to leave my job on that day, but I didn't. Although I had started painting on the side during nights and weekends, I hadn't yet begun to sell art. The idea of being a working artist still felt impossible. Though my student loans were finally paid off, now I had mortgage payments, a furniture wish list, and dreams of starting a family. The golden handcuffs tightened, and I continued working at Salomon Brothers and putting up with the bullshit of my male superiors for several more years.

My department was headed by two senior managers: an academic and a corporate hack. Mr. PhD hid in his corner office and left the day-to-day management to Tom, known for hiring pretty, petite women. One cold December night, Tom summoned me back to Lower Manhattan, immediately after an hour-long commute home to New Jersey. A huge client had gone belly-up in a derivatives-fueled fiasco.[6] I was the only analyst available who understood the computer models that priced these mysterious financial instruments, and they needed me for an emergency all-nighter to run numbers. The only woman there, I sat shoulder to shoulder with the men on the trading room floor. Around two or three in the morning, hovering behind me, Tom joked, "Maybe Miriam should take her shirt off to keep the rest of us awake."

His off-color remark that night was neither his first nor his last. Fortunately, my other manager, Mr. PhD, kept the overall tone of working there more civil, though he rarely bore witness to the worst that Tom offered up. Buried in his corner office, this economist famously wrote the formulas that fueled our most profitable proprietary trades. Therefore, it was no surprise when he joined Meriwether and his merry band of bond traders for their shiny new hedge fund in Greenwich, Connecticut.

THE FIRM

One by one, each of Meriwether's elite traders left our New York office and headed for the new firm in Greenwich. They were joined by industry veterans and respected economists from top business schools from Berkeley to Harvard. I imagined that if I worked for these brainy intellectuals, I'd escape the worst of Wall Street for a more simpatico situation. After calculating the commute from New Jersey to Greenwich, I sent my resume for one of their research analyst positions. Seduced by a six-figure salary and promises of a managerial role, I traded my Ann Taylor suits for business casual. Manager Tom was replaced by Tim,[7] who didn't *sexually* harass me but made sure my managerial role never materialized,[8] and I moved closer to the belly of the whale.

With double-digit returns in the first three years, the hedge fund rewarded us with lavish bonuses (which we were expected to invest *back into the firm's fund*) and extravagant trips. Shortly after I had arrived there, the partners flew the entire research team to London for on-site training. About a dozen of us were put up in Le Meridien, arguably one of London's best hotels. At the end of the following week, both the Greenwich and London teams were flown to the French Alps for a ski weekend. After two weeks away from my new husband, I asked a junior partner, Jay, if I could bow out early. Jay had been instrumental in recruiting me for my new job and insisted I go on the ski trip; he thought leaving early wouldn't be "a good look."

On this trip, we were divided into small groups based on our skill level. Jay and Sam, one of the more senior of the firm's founding partners, led our motley crew of nonskiing skiers. While waiting in a very long line for a lift, we spotted a second one with virtually no one waiting. When we finally reached the top, we learned why the line was so short. It was a black diamond trail. If you're not familiar with ski terminology, they assign color codes to designate the difficulty of each trail. A black diamond trail is a narrow, steep, rocky run with boulder drops to challenge more advanced skiers, assuming they don't mind the screaming. I took one look at it and announced, "I'm taking off my skis and walking down."

Except this was "The Firm." I put the words in quotation marks to conjure up the 1993 Tom Cruise movie, *The Firm*, in which Cruise plays a Harvard Law School graduate recruited to work for a prestigious law firm, only to learn that it has a dark, sinister side. Loyalty to The Firm (both the fictional version and my hedge fund) was expected above all else. In the culture of The Firm, you work, even if there's a terrorist attack. You sacrifice sleep for money. And certainly, you show that you're a team player by skiing a trail way beyond your skill level. With harassment far more insidious than what I had come to expect on the trading room floor, Sam and Jay insisted that I ski my way down the mountain.

The more evolved part of me now wishes I had held my boundary and walked down the mountain with my skis and head held high, exactly as I had retreated down those thirty-seven flights of stairs during the '93 World Trade Center bombing. However, by that point I'd been groomed to tolerate such abuse. Sexual and domestic abusers groom their victims through intentional manipulation to a point where they can be victimized. Abuse in the professional work world often happens the same way.

Professional abuse goes beyond the sexual harassment that makes headlines. Fat paychecks and benefits groom corporate workers to tolerate an abusive job or one not aligned with their values or life purpose. These are the golden handcuffs that tether us. Sam and Jay didn't harass me sexually, but they badly abused the power dynamic. After two weeks of being treated to five-star hotels and dinners on the town, I allowed them to *watch* as I wiped out over and over, tumbling the entire way down. I never forgave them for their hazing, and this experience planted seeds of doubt.

A few years later, it was my turn to watch these traders take a tumble down the mountain. Their fall came in the summer of 1998, when the once almighty hedge fund imploded, losing billions of dollars. Unlike the 1993 bombing of the World Trade Center, everyone in our office stopped working. Not only were our jobs on the line, but since we had been pressured to invest our bonuses back into the fund, many of us were in financial jeopardy as well. I personally lost over $30,000 of my salary.

During the meltdown, our office routine became the following: show up, pretend to work, drink two bottles of wine over lunch, gossip about what we thought would happen, and check the newswires to learn what was happening in our own company. Just like the terrorist attack of 1993, management wouldn't tell us the truth, nor could we read their poker faces. However, we knew things were bad when the partners started wearing neckties to work.[9]

The Firm wasn't the only institution in jeopardy. Since Long-Term Capital Management traded with every major bank using complex derivatives, our failure could cause a catastrophic economic meltdown. As a result, the Federal Reserve deemed us "too big to fail" and arranged for a buyout. The takeover team required a skeleton crew of employees to slowly unwind all our positions. Layoffs were imminent, especially in my vulnerable department.

By this time, I had a one-year-old daughter with whom I desperately wanted to spend more time—but my husband and I had no plan for how to make our mortgage payments without my salary. I decided to take a gamble of my own and offered to work part-time at reduced pay. The partners agreed, but with each passing month there was less work for me to do.

Now it was my turn to mask my emotions. All I had to do was show up and not draw attention to myself, and I could continue collecting a still-hefty paycheck. It may sound like a dream to be paid lots of money to pretend to work, but the lack of *meaning* in my days gradually crushed my soul. Worse yet, it began to feel as though I was getting paid to stay away from my daughter. I knew I wasn't living my life purpose. Pregnant with my second child, I gave two weeks' notice and walked away from that world for the last time.

RESISTING THE CALL

When I quit the hedge fund, a small part of me thought I might return someday. This reluctance to leave the ordinary world for a more extraordinary life is a common motif in literature, known as the hero's journey. This is a storytelling pattern common across time and cultures, from *The Wizard of Oz* and *Harry Potter* to *Star Wars.* Joseph Campbell first described this plot structure in his book *The Hero with a Thousand Faces.* In every story that follows this pattern, the hero feels a call to adventure. For example, Dorothy longs to go over the rainbow. Harry's calling is to become a wizard. Luke Skywalker feels called to join the Jedi Order. The typical hero in this storytelling genre will then resist the call. For example, Dorothy returns to her Aunt Em before the tornado carries her house away, and Harry doesn't believe he is in fact a wizard.

impostor syndrome the persistent inability to believe that one's success is deserved or has been legitimately achieved as a result of one's own efforts or skills

If you've ever thought "I don't feel like a real artist," please know that at some point we've all thought this. This lack of belief in your own identity is known as *impostor syndrome.* A variation of impostor syndrome is, "Who am I to _____?"; this fear usually goes hand in hand with the fear "What will they think?" All these unhelpful thoughts feed the starving-artist mentality. In a 2018 interview, psychotherapist and trauma-informed leadership coach Rebecca Bass-Ching shared with me: "At the heart of impostor syndrome is shame and scarcity mindset. If anyone dares to push growth edges and put themselves out of their comfort zone, then these protective narratives will always show up. No one is immune." If you want to make it as an artpreneur, you'll need to develop a mindset of abundance, and listen to the voices of inspiration rather than the voices of fear.

As creatives, we hear those whispers from the universe asking us to answer the call, and our resistance to taking that leap of faith is a refusal to answer. Art is a calling to align your life's purpose with your craft. Becoming an artist isn't much different from Harry Potter becoming a wizard. Your wand is your paintbrush, your pen, your camera, your computer, your instrument, or whatever tool you have chosen to wield. Creating something with the power of your imagination is magic.

If you resist answering the call, you're not alone. At first, even our favorite heroes resist the call. They may feel bound by some obligation to remain at home, or perhaps feel apprehensive about the unknown. The ties to your ordinary life keep you from acting on your dreams. What are the obligations preventing you from answering the call? Sometimes these obligations are tangible and tough to get around—especially for women, who traditionally bear the burden of caregiving, whether it's for their young children or their aging parents. According to an AARP study, the average caregiver is a forty-nine-year-old woman who spends nearly twenty hours a week providing unpaid care for her parents.[10] The expectation for women to carry society's burden pressures us to subjugate our own dreams in order to indulge those of others.

Although many of us have seasons in our lives that make change difficult, often the biggest burden we carry is our own indecision. Our discomfort with change encourages us to spend more time "thinking about it" until we "feel ready"—which only leads to additional anxiety about starting. "Thinking about it" just gives our brains more time to come up with unhelpful stories about why the dream of dedicating ourselves to our craft won't work. The fear that prevents us from going all-in on our dream is the greatest barrier to our achieving success.

I understand that resistance. When I broke up with my former job, I wasn't entirely convinced that I had left that world forever. In fact, a year after I left the hedge fund, I had thoughts of returning to my former world. My daughter was about to begin her second year of nursery school, and although I loved this immersion into motherhood, the tedium of my days left me longing for the glamour of Wall Street. I had begun dabbling in my art, but I hadn't yet created a compelling vision for my future. At that point it was easier to imagine trading in my spit-up-stained sweatshirts for the comfort of a regular paycheck. But then I had a wake-up call.

CROSSING THE THRESHOLD

It's normal to feel the pull to return to your ordinary world. But in both fiction and life, the greatest character growth occurs when the hero *cannot* return. In the hero's journey framework, the author often inserts a pivotal moment that makes turning back impossible. For example, the tornado carries Dorothy in her house away to Oz; and Luke's home planet is destroyed. In each of these stories, a cataclysmic event destroys the ordinary world or makes it impossible for the hero to return. For many creatives, losing a "safe" job can serve as this moment. For example, Faye, whom we met in the last chapter, was furloughed from her job during the coronavirus pandemic. For me, 9/11 made the return unimaginable.

A WAKE-UP CALL

Watching the World Trade Center burn on television brought flashbacks of 1993. During the nearly twenty minutes that passed between the first and second planes hitting their respective towers, there were no attempts to evacuate any of the nearby buildings. As I watched the news in horror, I muttered over and over, "That could've been me." I remembered my Salomon Brothers coworkers glued to their desks during the '93 bombing. And that night, I watched the traumatic meltdown of 7 World Trade Center, where Salomon Brothers had been the "anchor" tenant. Fortunately, nobody was in *that* building when it collapsed, just before five thirty that night—but I fully understood why thousands of people in the Twin Towers lost their lives. For those on the uppermost floors of the first tower, there was of course no way out. However, many others who *could* have gotten out, didn't.

Again, at places like Salomon Brothers or LTCM, a culture that made you ski down a treacherous black diamond slope that was well beyond your skill level also kept you working even during a terrorist attack. The same people who might carelessly wager a million dollars, or a finger, would wager your life. When I watched those towers collapse, I knew for a fact that I was never going to return. Not then. Not when my new baby started school. Not ever. And on that day, I decided I would do something different with my life.

WHAT ARE YOU WILLING TO SACRIFICE FOR YOUR "SAFE" JOB?

Your brain has evolved for survival and helps keep you "safe" from the perceived dangers that await outside your cave. However, we often choose to ignore the dangers *inside* the cave. Our fear of the unknown causes us to tolerate everything that's not working in our present situation. For the corporate worker (and particularly for women in corporate jobs), this can include misogyny, microaggressions, sexual harassment, systemic racism, being passed over for promotion, insufficient workplace boundaries, long hours, and more. But if we don't believe that a more extraordinary life awaits us, we hold on to our ordinary lives with all our might—even when we're being abused.

Right now, you may believe that staying in a job is more secure. But if the global pandemic has taught us anything, it's that "secure" jobs can change on a dime. When you work for someone else, there's always a risk that your job won't be as secure as you imagine. And with the comfort and security of your job perpetually on the line, is sticking it out really your better option? If you want to make it as an artpreneur, *you must take charge of your destiny.*

You might already be sensing that call to steer your own ship. During the pandemic, millions of artisans took charge of their own destinies by opening online stores. Etsy saw a 42 percent spike in new sellers in the third quarter of 2020,[11] pushing the total number of Etsy sellers to nearly four million.[12] By the first quarter of 2022, the number of Etsy sellers swelled to five million.[13] And even as the pandemic receded, businesses struggled to fill vacancies when the "quit rate" increased, leading economists to dub this era "the Great Resignation."[14] There's nothing like a crisis to lift the veil from whatever isn't working in your life. Maybe it's a commute you dread, or office politics, or maybe you're just left wondering, "Is this my life's purpose?"

THE TIME IS NOW

As you stand at the threshold between your ordinary life and the more extraordinary life that awaits you, don't wait for the next disaster as a sign from the universe. If you've been waiting for the right time to start a new creative career, or to even start making time for your creativity, please know that there will *never* be a perfect time. And I don't know one person who began their creative journey or a creative career who didn't wish they'd started it sooner. I have dedicated my life's work to creating resources to help you—like this book. Read on. The time to commit to your creativity is now.

A GUIDE APPEARS

Though you're the hero of your story, you're not alone. All heroes need and get help. Harry had Dumbledore. Luke had Obi-Wan. During our journey together, you might shake your head and think, "I'm not ready," or "It's not a good time"—but I'm here to arm you with the magical sword that will help you slay those mindset monsters and provide you with the practical knowledge you'll need to make all of this work. I'll be your guide as we deep dive into how to strengthen your belief in what's possible for *you*.

Meanwhile, keep a watchful eye on your thoughts. Here's a list of artists' most common thought distortions, along with more empowering replacement thoughts that you can use to practice thinking like a successful artpreneur.

THOUGHT WORK

STARVING ARTISTS THINK	ARTPRENEURS BELIEVE
X I'm not ready yet.	✔ I'm ready for the next step.
X It's not a good time.	✔ It's my time.
X This won't work for me because _____.	✔ The universe has my back.[15]
X I don't know how to _____.	✔ I'm figuring this out. I can't wait to figure this out.
X I've never done this before.	✔ I'm just beginning.
X This is hard.	✔ I like to accomplish things, even when they're hard.

WHAT ARTPRENEURS NEED TO BELIEVE

- Our fear of the unknown leads us to tolerate everything that's not working in our present situation.
- Art is a calling.
- Creating something with the power of your imagination is *magic*.

MARCHING ORDERS

- Always remember that you're the hero of your own story.
- When you find yourself hesitating at the threshold, it's normal to feel the pull to return to the ordinary world. Push through that hesitation and take a step closer toward your goals.
- Don't wait for a sign from the universe to pursue what matters most to you.

"WHETHER YOU SUCCEED OR NOT IS IRRELEVANT. . . . MAKING YOUR UNKNOWN KNOWN IS THE IMPORTANT THING."

—GEORGIA O'KEEFFE

3

START BEFORE
YOU'RE READY

MY HEART WAS RACING AS the sun set toward the red-and-green landscape. I had arrived at the dude ranch in New Mexico a few days earlier with a suitcase full of art supplies for a painting retreat: a gift to myself—a week to fully immerse in my art without the competing demands of teenage kids. Impulsively, I'd added an optional tour of Georgia O'Keeffe's home at Ghost Ranch—via horseback. As I stood awaiting my turn, I felt my stomach turning.

At the time of this retreat, I'd been living in New York for twenty-five years, and the last time I'd ridden a horse before that was in the fifth grade. My mom had signed me up for Girl Scout camp, but the horse bit me on the first day, and I discovered I was allergic to hay. (Not a fun summer.) Sure, I love to exercise, and I have a sense of adventure, but I'm a city slicker through and through and don't even own a proper pair of boots. (Not even the fake, trendy kind you see in catalogs.) So, when the good-looking cowboy called my name and told me to climb the platform, no part of me felt ready. And it didn't help that the British woman in front of me had asked the tour guide whether we'd be "trotting."

Don't you need lessons for this sort of thing? And why the heck do we need to climb up to get on this horse? What happened to the smaller ponies?

I didn't feel prepared. I didn't feel *ready*. But O'Keeffe's ranch is only accessible via horseback, and I sensed that this was a once-in-a-lifetime opportunity. I didn't want to miss out and regret not seeing it. When I finally mounted that horse, I took a deep breath and decided that my sweaty palms and I would go through with the ride—even though no part of me felt ready. It took the entire ride to settle my nerves, but, as you might imagine, it was the best part of my whole week in New Mexico.

Every successful artist starts before they're ready. They show up to the studio even when they feel uninspired. They send that marketing email even when they don't feel motivated. The inspiration comes from creating the art. The motivation comes from doing the work. The confidence comes from riding the wild horse of fear even when your brain tells you it's a bad idea. The reason you don't feel ready is because readiness isn't a feeling. You're feeling scared, unmotivated, or uninspired, but the story your brain tells you is that you're "just not ready yet."

SAY YES TO ADVENTURE

My decision to follow through on the horse trail ride enabled me to see the hills and the juniper that O'Keeffe once painted—and, along the way, to feel the energy of her spirit. As a result, I came home inspired—with new ideas and, more importantly, confidence. Starting before I feel ready is a habit that has served me well on the road to becoming a full-time artpreneur. Without it, I never would have quit my Wall Street job, launched a podcast, created online art classes, or even written this book. You may never *feel* ready, but you'll never get past that if you listen to the voice of doubt. As you'll soon see, your success won't hinge on getting rid of your fears but on acting despite them.

Those first few steps are scary. On my horseback ride, the hardest part was leaving the corral and crossing the first ditch that led to the path. My fears left me imagining that we were about to navigate the Grand Canyon. Of course, it was nothing like that. The ditch was just a three-foot-wide gully—and in moving forward, I felt more confident with every step.

THE FASTEST WAY TO BUILD CONFIDENCE

Most people assume you need confidence *before* you face scary steps and take big risks. But confidence isn't the same as fearlessness; you can be both confident and wary at the same time. I've found that the fastest way to build confidence is to act—to move ahead with the new things even when I don't feel ready. As you follow through with your commitments, you'll come to trust yourself and know that you've got your own back. This will build your confidence.

confidence
full trust; belief in the powers, trustworthiness, or reliability of a person or thing

So, do what you say you're going to do— even when you don't feel like it. As you can see from the prior definition, it's the trust that enables confidence. And it's a virtuous cycle. Confidence breeds trust—and the more you trust yourself, the more confident you become. Following through with an action plan builds your confidence. That's why when people follow through on a weight-loss program, they build confidence. They may think the greater confidence stems from their slimmer body, but the confidence boost actually comes from having followed through on their commitments, such as eating what they say they'll eat, and going to the gym when they say they will. (Meaning, you can build your confidence without giving up carbs.)

BUILDING TRUST

If you commit to doing the work of creating marketing content for your art, you'll gain confidence even if it doesn't lead to an immediate sale. Again, confidence comes from learning to trust yourself, and the first step toward trustworthiness is doing what you say you're going to do. In addition, this is also a fast way to gain the trust of the people to whom you're selling. My podcast listeners know that I release a new *Inspiration Place* episode every Tuesday and have done so without fail since I started the podcast in August 2018. They can count on it. This quickly develops listener loyalty, which makes it easier for them to trust me and then value investing in my programs. You can also develop this relationship with your prospects by sending out regular emails and committing to creating and publishing weekly content, such as blog posts, social media posts, or videos.

THE BELIEF TRIAD

To be a successful artpreneur, you must fully commit to all three points of the belief triad.

1. Believe in and love *your art*.
2. Believe in *yourself* (and call yourself an artist).
3. Believe in *your buyer*: the art collector, customer, or client.

If you're struggling to make a full-time living as an artpreneur, it's because you have limiting beliefs in one or more of these areas. If you don't believe in your talent, you'll lack belief in your art. If you don't believe in your ability to sell or market your art, that reflects a lack of belief in yourself. And if you believe in your art and yourself but *still* don't think there's an audience for your work willing to pay for it, that's a lack of belief in your buyer.

Understand the power of the belief triad so you can start questioning your limiting beliefs. Get in the habit of recognizing your own limiting beliefs as we unpack the inspired action steps you'll need to take.

BEWARE THE LIMITS OF MAGICAL THINKING

Though what I'm sharing about the belief triad shares similarities with the "Law of Attraction" theory, there are crucial differences. I'm going to share the latter's framework, and, in comparison, I'll soon show how my approach is grounded in brain science.

Rhonda Byrne's bestselling book *The Secret* led readers to conclude that, if you believe hard enough, everything you want will materialize. Want a Ferrari? Believe hard enough, and it will appear in your driveway. Byrne has not been alone in her presentation. Many Law of Attraction theorists advocate that all you have to do is believe fully enough, and you can have anything your heart desires. However, this idea is often presented without the critical step of taking *inspired action*. Yes, you must believe with total commitment, but you won't get the results you want without taking inspired action. The action you take from the place of belief makes all the difference.

Keep in mind that there's a difference between *inspired* action and *desperate* action. When our actions are inspired, they come from a confident place, and they'll be in alignment with confident beliefs. When we act from a place of scarcity, our actions are less effective because customers sense our desperation. Confidence is magnetic. Desperation is repelling. You must show up in the world with "hot girl" energy. Hot girls (a nongendered term popularized by American rapper Megan Thee Stallion) are unapologetically confident in themselves and Hot girls show up with a completely different energy than those who are desperate.[1]

GET OUT OF YOUR OWN WAY

Mind management is grounded in cognitive behavioral therapy, an extension of psychotherapy founded in the 1960s by psychiatrist Dr. Aaron Beck.[2] Beck recognized that a person's perception of a situation has a greater effect on their mindset than the situation itself. As a result, instead of exploring the root source of the anxiety, his method of therapy focuses on changing the unhelpful thinking. Here we're going to explore the unhelpful thinking that may be sabotaging your results. Once you learn to change the way you think, you'll get out of your own way and produce better outcomes.

YOUR BRAIN WANTS YOU SAFE

There's nothing wrong with you if you're harboring unhelpful thoughts that are holding you back—so if anything I present here sounds like you, don't worry or beat yourself up. Your brain's job is to perpetuate thoughts that keep you alive and unharmed, which is why it has a negativity bias.[3] We humans have evolved this way as it has enabled the survival of our species. As a result, your brain knows that when you feel comfortable, you're safe. Anytime you enter new, unfamiliar territory, your brain gets uncomfortable and will rebel!

Your brain doesn't know the difference between the threat inherent in leaving your cave in the middle of the night and that of offering your art for sale. Even though someone saying no to buying your art won't hurt you physically, your brain can't distinguish between fear of rejection and fear of man-eating tigers. So, all new situations activate the part of the brain that generates fear—the barometer that indicates danger is near. In order to calm your fear, your brain comes up with all manner of reasons why a new (uncomfortable!) situation won't work for you, or why you're "not ready yet."

DOUBTS, NOT EXCUSES

I've heard other business coaches shame and blame their clients for "making excuses." I don't use the word "excuses" because the fears behind your reasons feel real to you. (Moreover, the smarter you are, the better your brain will be at generating unhelpful thoughts.) Let's call these thoughts *doubts* instead. Still, they're unhelpful, which, left unchecked, will hold you back. These doubts often make us confused about the "correct" action to take next. Sometimes people get so confused that they doubt the viability of any action at all. Others will go into what I call "procrasti-learning" mode and bury themselves in the research stage. Procrasti-learning stems from a sense of perfectionism—they just want to get it "right," but all the extra information overwhelms them with more fear and more doubt, especially when they find conflicting advice. Should you self-publish, or try getting an agent? Should you sell your art online, or get gallery representation? Who knows? Might as well have another latte!

WHY YOU PROCRASTI-ANYTHING

Whether you don't know how to move forward, or you've spent endless hours researching the "right" way, the result is usually *not* taking any action. Researching makes you feel like you're doing something, but learning without acting doesn't help you. When you're confused and overwhelmed, most likely you won't take any actions that will advance your business (but there's a good chance you'll end up in front of the pantry, looking for a snack: procrasti-snacking). Why *should* you act? If you aren't clear what the correct next step is, then it seems to make sense *not* to act. Sound familiar?

procrasti-learning

using research to justify

postponing action

MANAGING YOUR MIND

Don't worry, grasshopper, I'll absolutely give you the exact steps you need to take to achieve the results you're seeking. But I wanted to warn you from the start that you need to be constantly vigilant about your thoughts. Many of the steps I suggest will make you uncomfortable just *thinking* about them. If you catch yourself thinking, "That won't work for me *because*..." know that this thought is most likely a story you're telling yourself, and that it won't serve you. As your guide for this journey, I'll keep sharing stories of artists just like you so you can recognize the most common limiting belief patterns.

BELIEVE IN YOURSELF

Garden-variety self-help books routinely talk about the importance of believing in yourself. What they don't do is address all three necessary components of the belief triad. First, you need to be sold on yourself. You need to believe in yourself. You must be buying yourself. Sell yourself on *you* before you sell anyone else on you or your art. If you're unwilling to believe in yourself, how could you even ask other people to believe in you? Not your partner, not your mother, not your best friends, and not your client, art collector, or the prospects on your email list.

If you aren't sold on *you*, you probably won't act on what I'm going to share here. Believe with all your heart that your effort is worth it and take action to move forward. Let go of the safety and ordinariness of your current life and believe that a more extraordinary life awaits you.

"A SHIP IN PORT IS SAFE. BUT THAT'S NOT WHAT SHIPS ARE BUILT FOR."

—GRACE HOPPER

BELIEVE IN YOUR ART

Alice Neel, born at the dawn of the twentieth century, wanted to be an artist, but her mother admonished, "I don't know what you expect to do in the world, Alice. You're only a girl."[4] Instead of accepting the severe limitations of the Victorian era her mother knew, Neel went off to study at the prestigious Philadelphia School of Design for Women with the help of scholarships and her savings from secretarial work.[5] She shared with art historian Cindy Nesmer, "[My mother's words], instead of destroying me, made me more ambitious because I'd think, you know, I'll show them, I'll show her, I'll show everybody."[6]

This is what 100 percent belief in yourself looks like, but more than that, Neel had 100 percent belief in her *art*. Throughout her career, she primarily chose figures as her subjects and painted in a quasi-impressionist style reminiscent of van Gogh's portraits. To the modern eye this may not seem like a brave choice, but Neel painted in New York throughout the 1950s when her contemporaries, such as Helen Frankenthaler and Jackson Pollock, were having success painting in the popular Abstract Expressionist style.

Neel's relentless commitment to her art paid off, and at the end of her life in 1984, she enjoyed a retrospective at the Whitney Museum of American Art. More recently, the 2021 blockbuster "People Come First" exhibition at the Metropolitan Museum of Art placed Neel and her art in the canon of art history.

Also in 2021, another woman, Ethiopian-born American artist Julie Mehretu, was celebrated with a solo show in New York, this time at the Whitney. While Neel favored figures and portraits over abstract art, Mehretu's large abstract canvases reflect a similarly unconventional choice. As a woman of color, the more obvious genre might have been figurative painting—with the popularity of Black figure painting on the rise since the Obamas commissioned Amy Sherald and Kehinde Wiley to paint their official portraits. Mehretu's choice to paint in an abstract style to communicate her ideas about social justice runs counter to what is expected or popular. Choosing to paint what's not in vogue takes 100 percent belief in your art.

LOVE YOUR ART!

Understand that regardless of the type of art you create—whether it's poetry, pottery, painting, sculpture, crafts, or any other form of self-expression—you must love your art so fiercely that you truly feel the world will miss out if they don't want what you're offering! Continue to take inspired action, creating your art and putting it out in the world no matter what—even when evidence suggests that your marketing may not be working.

BELIEVE IN YOUR BUYER

Though most business advice recommends believing in yourself or your product (in this case, your art), few marketing experts talk about the importance of believing in the third part of the belief triad: your buyer.

In the 1990 movie *Pretty Woman*, Julia Roberts agrees to be Richard Gere's ladylike companion for his event-packed business week in Beverly Hills. In order to look the part, he hands her his Gold Card with instructions to buy whatever she wants. When Roberts heads to Rodeo Drive in cheap, provocative attire, the boutique salespeople don't trust that she has the means to purchase anything and refuse to wait on her. After a more successful shopping spree, spending an obscene amount of money at other stores, Roberts returns to the offending boutique. This time she's dressed to the nines and loaded with shopping bags. Smugly, she asks the dismissive salespeople whether they work on commission, and when they say they do, she responds, "*Big* mistake."

As a customer, I've been on the receiving end of a salesperson who didn't believe in my ability to buy, and it felt icky. Developing belief in your buyer is critical. Unfortunately, a lack of belief in the customer happens all the time, and if you tell yourself unhelpful stories about what your buyer is thinking, you'll sabotage your results. So, how do you know if your imagination is defeating you? Perhaps you've said to yourself some version of the following:

Starving-Artist Thought Distortions

"No one buys art in my town/area/state/country."

"There are too many artists in Australia/Florida/New York/Boise, Idaho."

"No one is buying art because there's a recession/pandemic/social justice movement/tsunami in Indonesia."

You might even tell contradictory stories. Like Judy, an artist I met, who shared: "Everyone moves down to Florida from New York.... People in Florida are so cheap and looking for a bargain.... People in Florida don't appreciate art like they do in New York."

Wait, what? You just told me everyone moves down to Florida from New York!

I've heard such stories a million times. "No one buys art in my town." "No one pays for art." Yet I can find evidence, both from my artist clients and my own experience, that people buy art all over the world, regardless of circumstances. Yes, in Florida. Yes, in Australia. Yes, in Idaho. Yes, in whatever state or country you live in. And with art available for purchase online, what does it matter where you live, anyway? Of course, another limiting belief I've heard is that people don't buy art *online*. Tell that to abstract painter Julie Mehretu, who sold a painting through the online marketplace Artsy for $6.5 million in June 2021, shattering all records for online auction sales and setting a new personal best for herself.

Ruminating on negative thoughts and telling yourself unhelpful stories about your customer is a big mistake. When you believe in your buyer, that means you're thinking positively about them. If you're having trouble recognizing what may be your unhelpful thoughts, doing a brain dump by journaling can help you root out unhelpful thinking. When you catch yourself thinking negatively, just ask yourself, "Is this really true?"—and look for evidence that the opposite may also be true.

REMEMBER:
THERE WILL NEVER BE A "RIGHT" TIME

Don't listen to the voice of doubt. Listen to that other voice, the creative whispers that encourage you to dream and *dream big*. Commit to being uncomfortable and taking a risk to move forward even if you don't feel ready, or you feel like it's not the right time. Know this: while the voice of doubt tells you it's not the right time, the truth is that there will never be a right time. Before those dreams turn to regrets, start today.

"YOU DON'T GET OLD UNTIL YOU REPLACE DREAMS WITH REGRETS."

—TROY DUMAIS

THOUGHT WORK

Part One: Growing an Abundance Mindset

Step 1: Write down your thoughts, including the good, the bad, and the ugly. This is a brain dump of whatever is on your mind, including everything you're thinking about yourself, your art, your prospects, and your personal life. Julia Cameron, in her book *The Artist's Way*, calls this practice "morning pages," but you can journal anytime you're feeling stuck. Her practice includes prompts for your writing, but you can just write down everything on your mind to clear the dust off.

Step 2: Label your thoughts. Do any of your statements fall into the category of all-or-nothing thinking? Were you mind reading or fortune-telling?

Step 3: Write down all the evidence *supporting* your thoughts. Is there a seed of truth? Even distorted thoughts often contain a seed of truth, which is why they take root in our minds.

Step 4: Write down the evidence *against* your thoughts. In which ways are your sabotaging thoughts false?

Step 5: Weed your thought garden. Pull out the thoughts you no longer want to believe, and plant more helpful ones. Once you begin questioning your preconditioned beliefs, you can start replacing the most common starving-artist thoughts with more empowering ones.

In the next thought work chart, you'll find the replacements for three types of negative thoughts, which will move you to become the confident artist that's your birthright.

Part Two: Transforming Thought Distortions

STARVING ARTISTS THINK	TYPE OF THOUGHT DISTORTION	ARTPRENEURS BELIEVE
X I'm not ready.	All-or-nothing thinking	✓ I'm ready for the next step.
X They don't want to pay.	Fortune-telling	✓ They are willing to pay me for my art. ✓ They want to collect art now.
X They don't have the money.	Fortune-telling	✓ They value art.
X People will copy/ steal images of my art.	Fortune-telling	✓ My art inspires others.
X I won't be able to sell any art.	Fortune-telling	✓ I am learning how to sell art.
X They don't like my art.	Mind reading	✓ They *love* my art.

X They don't like me.	Mind reading	✓ They want to work with me.
X It's not worth the effort.	All-or-nothing thinking	✓ My art is worth the effort.
X No one buys art in my town/area/ state/country.	All-or-nothing thinking	✓ Art is sold all over the world.
X There are too many artists in Australia/ Florida/New York/ Boise, Idaho.	All-or-nothing thinking	✓ There are enough customers for everyone.
X No one is buying art because there's a recession/ pandemic/social justice movement/ tsunami in Indonesia.	All-or-nothing thinking	✓ Art is needed in all times. ✓ The world needs art. ✓ The world needs *my* art.

WHAT ARTPRENEURS NEED TO BELIEVE

- The belief triad consists of three points: belief in yourself, your art, and your buyer.
- Inspired actions come from thinking empowering thoughts.
- Alternatively, when you think starving-artist thoughts, your actions will be less effective.

MARCHING ORDERS

- Write down your thoughts on a regular basis to examine what you're thinking.
- Pull out the thoughts you no longer want to believe, and plant more helpful ones.

"AND THE TROUBLE IS,
IF YOU DON'T RISK ANYTHING,
YOU RISK MORE."

—ERICA JONG

TAKE THE FIRST STEP

I REACHED UP ON MY TIPPY toes to staple the bright orange con-
struction paper to the top of the bulletin board in front of the
student center. Atop the orange rectangle, I offset a yellow flier
advertising the student center's comedy night. The colors reflected the New England fall foliage on campus. I'd applied
there because my father (who had passed away when I was five
years old) was an alumnus. I hoped the admissions officers
would look past my less-than-stellar grades and focus on my
heartbreaking essay about my dysfunctional childhood—and
they did. Student loans, scholarships, and my mother's savings
barely covered the costs. Fortunately, for extra spending money,
part of my college's financial-aid package included work-study.

Work-study is a fantastic program that provides grants to pay
students who seek employment from anywhere on campus. In
my mind, the least ingenious of my classmates settled for jobs in
the cafeteria, while the luckiest got to work in the library, where
they could do their homework while working. One of my best
work-study jobs was working at the student center's information
desk. I loved it because throughout my shift I could scope out

students who were too cool to eat at the cafeteria and instead chose Collis, the student center's trendy vegetarian café. Unfortunately, I quickly used up many of my dining dollars there. To keep up the pricey lentil loaf habit, I often skipped breakfast and grabbed a free donut at art history faculty lectures.

My student center job included decorating the bulletin board that advertised campus events. At the same time, I had volunteered to be the "publicity" chair for the governing board that planned these events, and this volunteer work included creating hand-lettered and -illustrated advertising posters. It seemed silly that the school paid me to hang the posters, but not to draw them. But then, through both my paid work at the information desk and my volunteer work with the student government, I learned that the college regularly paid professional commercial artists (not students) to design most of their promotional materials. I wanted a piece of that; but first I had to be brave enough to speak up and ask.

HUNGER GIVES YOU COURAGE

I didn't need courage to fuel me. I was annoyed that I was volunteering to do work that commercial artists got paid to do. I petitioned to apply my work-study money toward getting paid for the volunteer work that my rich classmates did for free. If I wanted to eat side by side with my classmates at Collis Café, I had to give up my role on the student governing board because otherwise I wouldn't be earning money for creating posters. (I wasn't allowed to both volunteer and be paid for the same position.) But that was okay by me. My classmates didn't need my opinion about the winter carnival theme. And I intended to make bank.

Fast-forward to these same classmates painting posters for their children's school PTAs and perhaps wondering why they can't make money from their art.

Offering your art and time for free is a choice. You can also choose to decide that you'll only provide art to others when you're compensated. To become an artpreneur, you must believe your art is worth paying for, and ask people to pay you. Yes, there are people out there waiting for you to show up and claim your value. You'll hear the word "no" many times along the way, but you'll be surprised by how often organizations have funds that can be allocated to enhance their projects with your creativity.

I never went to art school, but I learned a more valuable lesson: people are willing to *pay* for art. In college, I might not have believed that I could turn my art into a full-time living, nor did I then appreciate how high the upper limit could be. (Hint: It's always higher than we think.) But ultimately, I was uncomfortable enough in my situation that I was willing to risk failure.

I want you to hunger for a more extraordinary life and let some people say "no" to *you*. Don't say "no" for them! If you do, you'll never get that "yes" you crave. Be hungry enough for that "yes" to risk failure along the way.

STEP ZERO

Moving forward feels scary. "Step zero" is finding the courage to monetize your creativity—and taking the practical steps that will ready you to receive money. Remember, finding courage doesn't mean having no fear. Courage is being afraid and deciding to act in spite of it.

courage

the ability to do something that frightens one

There's no need to feel fully confident before you start asking for sales. Confidence is a choice to set an intention. Step zero is just setting an intention to monetize your creativity. No need to feel ready or get rid of that fear first!

Assigning a value to your art and asking others to pay that full value feels uncomfortable, and this is normal. But you can reach a point where the discomfort of staying stuck outweighs your discomfort with changing. When I was in college, the discomfort of struggling on financial aid and wanting more income to keep up with the lifestyle of my wealthier classmates fueled that desire. After I left Wall Street, my determination not to return to the corporate world continued to motivate me.

KNOW WHAT YOU REALLY WANT

Ask yourself: How much do I want to earn from my business? When I speak to artists who don't have money goals, I spend a good part of our time coaching them on believing what's possible for them, and then attaching a number to their goal. In addition, if a prospective client shares that they don't care about the money, I won't work with them. To make money from your art, you need to *want* it—and money doesn't go where it isn't wanted.

Recently, I coached a client named Sara. She was gearing up for a three-day art show, and I wanted her to get clear on her goals. When I asked what she wanted from the show, she admitted she "hoped to collect some emails and sell some prints." When I pushed her to get more specific and create a bigger goal, she resisted. She felt that setting a bigger goal could bring disappointment. But with a wishy-washy goal, she doomed herself to mediocre results. This is very common, and in the past, you might have set unambitious goals for yourself to avoid disappointment. That's got to stop. You're not going to go any further than your goal, and if your goal is too modest, it will limit you.

On the other hand, not having a goal at all is like driving your car aimlessly until you run out of gas. You should even set the goal *beyond* the goal so that your upper limit is high. The best way to explain the concept of a goal beyond the goal is with my grandfather's favorite quote by Robert Browning: "Ah, but a man's reach should exceed his grasp."[1] You'll want to create a goal that makes you feel excited, since those feelings will motivate your actions. Remember, your thoughts generate feelings that fuel your actions, which ultimately drive your results. That's why it's important to monitor your thoughts—to make sure they'll lead to the outcome you're looking for. Big goals generate positive energy to make your art career soar.

"HOW DO I PRICE MY ART?"

Pricing art is very subjective and often feels arbitrary. So many factors determine a sufficient price: the venue, materials, subject, presentation, affluence of your market, and so on. Regardless of what you're selling, if you're willing to make mistakes as you find your pricing path, you'll learn faster than wanting to get everything perfect in advance. You'll always make faster progress when you're willing to make mistakes along the way. We'll dive deeper into pricing and buyer psychology in chapter 7, but for now I want you to see the big picture of how pricing fundamentals come together.

Be Willing to Ask

Let's say you want to sell T-shirts. (This is just an example—you can replace the T-shirt with anything you create.) Up until now, you've been giving them away at charity events. You have no idea how to make this into a business because you've never priced your T-shirts. Someone you met at a charity event now wants to buy one of your shirts. What do you charge?

A T-shirt might seem reasonable at $10 or even over $100. To test that theory, I did a quick search on Bergdorf Goodman's website for black T-shirts. I chose black T-shirts as an example because they come in a range of prices, and I wanted to see how the prices could differ based on venue, design, and materials. For this search, I found a plain, short-sleeved, black T-shirt priced at $120. Then I did a second search for black T-shirts on the

Neiman Marcus site and found Givenchy men's tees priced at $455.[2] In both cases, the high-end department stores recognize that luxury buyers equate a high price tag with greater value. Now let's imagine that Brandon Maxwell, Lady Gaga's designer, custom-made a black T-shirt just for you. What would you expect to pay for it? There are countless answers on how to price a simple black T-shirt—yet all are correct if the seller is willing to *ask* and if there's a desire match with the right buyer.

Be Willing to Receive

Taking the first step is all about your willingness to ask. If you want to make money from your art, you must ask for the sale *and* be ready to receive the abundance. If you don't believe there's an audience willing to pay you, be mindful of the ways you might sabotage yourself with your limiting beliefs about money.

Limiting beliefs creep in with artists at all levels, including those who have been selling for a while but have trouble raising their prices. Most people block abundance when they don't feel worthy of receiving it. Many people, particularly women and people of marginalized groups, have been conditioned not to desire money (or sex and power!).[3] Cultural programming and social conditioning (along with lived experiences) have convinced them that it isn't safe to want these things or that they're wrong for wanting them. To break free of the starving-artist archetype, be willing to receive abundance and recognize that it's both okay and safe to desire money for your art.

Embrace Risk

To get started in any business, start asking people to pay you. If you believe starting is any more complicated than that, then you're not telling yourself the truth about what's holding you back: *fear.* Whether you're afraid of failing or afraid of succeeding, you're imagining an outcome that makes you uncomfortable—and it's your comfort with where you are now that keeps you from taking risks.

Before taking step zero, people sometimes ask me to give them baby steps to take so they won't fall along the way. Unfortunately, it doesn't work that way. No matter how good your strategy is, you won't be willing to implement it until you're willing to embrace failure. Nobody gets from zero to ten in reaching any goals without falling down a few times. Think about the athletes who are the greatest in their fields yet still fall while preparing to compete in the Olympics. To make any progress, you must be willing to fail.

For the attitude you need, think about how babies learn to walk. They fall down every step of the way. (And when they do, no one says, "Hey, maybe this walking thing just isn't for you.") That attitude of embracing failure in order to progress is exactly what you need when you create a business.

+ + + **MINDSET CHECK-IN** + + +

Write down all your fears about asking people to pay for your creativity. *All* of them. Each sentence you write is a thought lurking in your mind. Are any of your sentences thought distortions?

When I journal, I use a shorthand with abbreviations for each type of thought distortion.

Mind reading = MR | Fortune-telling = FT
All-or-nothing thinking = AON

Labeling your thoughts will help you notice the ones that don't serve you.

PRACTICAL STEPS FOR
SETTING UP YOUR BUSINESS

Let's dive into some practical aspects of setting up your art business. Many folks believe the first thing they need to do is print business cards, design a logo, or create an LLC. However, there's one thing you must have before anything else. Can you guess what that is? Nope, it isn't a website (although you'll need one). The very first thing you need to make your art business real is a *business bank account* completely separate from your personal bank accounts. When you're in business, you must have a way to receive and spend money to run it. Even if you have the bare minimum of overhead (your art supplies, website, and more), you don't want to muck that all up by mixing your business expenses with personal ones. Your business bank account gives you both a financial *and* a mental container for receiving money for your art.

Your business bank account suite includes your checking account (just for the business), a savings account (also for the business), and a credit card (again, used only for the business). After I sold my first portrait, I marched over to the local bank to open a business account. The bank manager who helped me said I'd get a free checking account as long as it was linked to the savings account with a minimum balance. This business bank account suite also included a no-fee credit card as part of the deal. For many years, I kept only the minimum balance in savings, but as my business grew I started keeping several months' operating expenses as well.

Your business bank account suite will allow you to receive and send money while keeping your business's financial records and decisions separate from your personal ones. Creating a business with these parameters facilitates better decision-making. For example, if you've got a life partner (whom you're not in business with), when you segregate your business and personal finances, you won't need to ask their permission to make business investments (even if you're so inclined). And separate accounts simplify decisions about big purchases, such as coaching, educational resources, or hiring an assistant.

Even with the most rudimentary of bookkeeping, keeping my art business finances separate enables me to instantly access how much revenue I've generated, what my profit is, and how much money I've got in my business checking account. I always know whether I have the money to invest back in my business after paying myself. And when I want money from my business, I can withdraw it and deposit it into my personal account or the joint checking account I share with my husband, or deposit it into the savings account I have for myself. But I never use my personal accounts to pay my business bills. This all means you're not paying for an Etsy shop with your personal account or paying personal bills with your business account. If you do, you'll have a nightmare of a time come tax season and you'll have trouble wrapping your head around business decisions.

March over to a bank and open a business checking account to make your business official. Once you do, you're ready for true artpreneurship.

MAKE YOUR ART BUSINESS "REAL"

Every dollar you spend is either for a business or personal expense. Every dollar you earn is business income. From now on, start classifying every dollar in your life as either business or personal. If you don't separate your personal and business money, you're going to have all sorts of problems.

Artists who don't track their finances feel out of control and unaware of how much money their business has. That's why they feel broke all the time, or they keep using their personal money to float the business—or, worse yet, asking their partner's *permission* to make new investments. Furthermore, none of your financial stats mean a thing until you're paying yourself. Consult an accountant to decide whether you should pay yourself with an "owner's draw" or an actual salary. Ultimately, know that money withdrawn from your business account for personal use is taxable income.

+ + + HERE'S THE RULE + + +

Create a business account, and a personal account, and keep them separate. Period. (They can even be in different banks. I use the same bank, but the accounts are not linked, so it's more difficult for me to transfer from one to the other.) Without this, you cannot become intentional about any investments of your personal money that you make in your business.

MINIMIZING DECISION DRAMA

Making decisions is hard! We waste so much time and energy "thinking about it." We can also lose money when we take too much time to make up our minds and miss opportunities. For example, my client Nancy was trying to decide between two studio spaces in downtown Chicago. One space cost $750 per month but was very inconvenient. The other was a short distance from her home but cost hundreds more. She was indecisive for so long that she lost out on the lower-priced one.

You make countless decisions to move forward in your life, your art, and your business. But when you don't decide, of course you don't have to risk failure. Keep in mind that your customers, too, are afraid to risk making mistakes—such as buying the wrong art. That's why the belief triad is a powerful tool. Projecting a strong belief about yourself and your art will help your customers worry less about making their own mistakes by investing in your art. When you're uncertain, you'll be projecting uncertainty, which will repel your customers. When you're confident, you'll be projecting certainty, which will make your customers feel more comfortable about buying from you.

OWN YOUR DECISIONS

One of the reasons for a knee-jerk response like "I have to ask my _____" is that you believe it lets you off the hook. When you get buy-in from someone else, you believe that if you fail, you can shift some of the blame to them. ("You told me you thought this was a good idea!") When you take 100 percent sovereignty over your decisions, you'll also become more accountable for their outcomes. As a result, you'll be more determined and driven to succeed. Choose to believe that every decision you make is the right one. Let me explain.

If you grew up in the early eighties or nineties, chances are you came across the Choose Your Own Adventure book series. These paperbacks, written in the second person, were considered children's gamebooks. As the main character of the book, the reader gets to direct the plot. With titles like *The Cave of Time* and *Mystery of the Maya*, the series bragged of forty possible different endings per book. Do you take a potion that takes you back in time or turn to page twenty-eight to search for a missing friend in present-day Mexico? Part of the fun of reading these books was flipping back to find out what would have happened if you'd made a different choice. In real life, unlike the Choose Your Own Adventure series, you usually never know what would have happened if you'd made a different choice. This means you'll never know if you made the "right" decision, because you'll never learn the outcome of a different choice.

Rather than spend your energy worrying about making the "right" decision or the "best" decision, which will send you down a rabbit hole of procrasti-learning and analysis paralysis, it's better to make a quick decision and invest your energy in committing to it. There's a reason why *Jeopardy!* champions credit quick buzzer skills as the key to their success. Being the first to hit the buzzer often means they're acting before they're absolutely sure of the answer. Rather than focusing on making perfect choices, spend your energy focusing on taking inspired actions and committing to the choices you've already made. There's no way of knowing for sure if you've ever made the right choice, so always assume you made the right decision and act from that place.

WHAT ARTPRENEURS NEED TO BELIEVE

- Offering your art and time for free is a choice.
- When you own your decisions, you become more accountable for their outcomes.
- Choosing to believe that every decision you make is the right one makes all the difference.
- A big goal generates the positive energy that makes your art career soar.

MARCHING ORDERS

- **Open a separate business checking account.** This should be a checking account with a linked savings account.
- **Track your income and expenses.** There are lots of online apps that make this super simple to automate.
- **Make it a habit to pay your business bills with business money only.** Mixing personal and business money gets messy fast. Also, business money withdrawn for personal use is taxable income.

- **Choose a website "builder" so that you can easily build a website using drag-and-drop technology.** Make sure the one you choose is set up for e-commerce, which will enable PayPal and credit card payments.
- **Create a Stripe account to accept credit cards.** (Your website provider will have instructions for integrating this service.)
- **Create PayPal, Venmo, and Zelle accounts so you have an alternate way to receive payments online.**

"FORGET REGRET,
    OR LIFE IS YOURS TO MISS."

                    —JONATHAN LARSON

FOCUS ON WHAT
MATTERS MOST

THE TAN, MUSCULAR, BLEACHED-BLONDE WOMAN strode to the front of the room, spun on her heel, and stared fiercely at the room full of instructors. Although Michelle's red spandex crop top and tight black biker shorts didn't match her serious demeanor, we knew she meant business.

The required training session was part of the curriculum for all new gym instructors. We had spent the morning learning the series of exercises that comprised the gym's signature-brand power workout. This session represented the first in a series with master trainers who shared their success secrets for rising to the top of the gym's power structure and commanding the highest hourly rates.

Michelle continued staring at us until the room fell silent, as we shifted uncomfortably in our chairs. She then held up a blue-and-white paperback and declared, "This book will change your life"—while pumping her other fist into the air. No, it wasn't a book on Pilates or weight training. The cover on the slim paperback read: *The Certifiable Salesperson.*[1] Raising an eyebrow, she added, "Sadly, most of you won't read it. You believe that your hot body will sell training packages." Sniffing a challenge, I scribbled the name of the book on my yellow legal pad.

At this time, I was painting on the side, but I hadn't yet gone all-in on an art career. Since I didn't want to go back to the corporate world, I started teaching Pilates at a big chain of gyms in the New York metropolitan area. The gym business model relies not only on memberships but also on upselling personal training packages to their clients. As a result, this gym chain invested a lot of time in training their new recruits in sales fundamentals.

Between Michelle and the next two trainers, I filled up several pages on my yellow pad. They all suggested that we add personal touches, like cards, gifts, or little bonuses, to keep customers coming back for more. They reviewed the anatomy of the sale, how to nurture client relationships, and the value of referrals. Fired up from a day of exercise and motivational talks, I hatched a plan to hook my next sale—but not for the gym.

On my way home from sales training, I popped into a bookstore inside Grand Central Station to buy the book that Michelle had recommended, and hungrily devoured it during the forty-five-minute commute home. This short book taught me that sales and marketing were skills anyone could learn. I figured traditional techniques could be used to sell *anything*, including art. Just as Michelle pointed out, it doesn't matter if you have a hot body (or amazing art): no matter what you're selling, sales require work. You can't just expect to make sales because you're awesome. However, if I was going to turn my energy toward marketing, I wanted my efforts to fuel my passion for art, not personal training packages.

I had recently painted a portrait of my four-year-old son, Seth, in his Batman suit. The watercolor painting captured his likeness and the bat-eared costume with the sculpted muscles added a bit of whimsy. The painting had even won a ribbon at a local juried show,[2] but ribbons don't sell art; people do. Seth loved the painting so much that he proudly showed it off to all his friends when they came over for playdates. My son "sold" the idea of getting your portrait painted to his friends. The kids were impressed by Seth's celebrity status captured in a painting and wanted one of themselves.

Strategically, I moved the framed painting into our foyer so his friends' parents would see the portrait when they came to pick up their kids. With the portrait in full view, Seth's friends remembered to ask their parents if Seth's mom could paint their portrait. Children are the best influencers. This sly bit of influencer marketing led to commissions, and then more people saw those portraits, leading to added referrals. Before I knew it, I had a full-time business painting portraits.

I made many rookie mistakes on my path to making it as an artpreneur, including starting commissions without getting a deposit first. Kim, a mom I met through my son's preschool, gave me a photo of their backyard, which overlooked the famed Winged Foot Golf Club. She planned to surprise her husband with the painting as a Father's Day gift. With the photo in my possession, the size and price finalized, I thought I was good to go and finished the painting.

When I bumped into Kim the next day, she informed me, "Hey, don't start that painting yet. I decided to give my husband a new set of golf clubs instead." With a poker face worthy of my Wall Street bosses, I replied, "Kim, my gallery would be happy to sell the painting if you don't want it." Her fear of missing out motivated her to whip out her checkbook on the spot and collect the painting after all. However, that was the last time I started a painting without first taking a deposit.

If I had any lingering doubts about my commitment to my art, the universe conspired to keep me out of the Pilates studio with an emergency appendectomy, followed by a broken toe. My love affair with portraits really kicked off during this time, and I continuously looked for ways to elevate my marketing. For example, whenever I sold a portrait to someone at my children's school, I delivered it at pickup time in the school parking lot so other moms would see it. I also gave my clients a note card set that featured their commission on the front. If my client referred me to a friend, I'd give them another set of blank note cards as a gift. Worth noting, giving a physical free gift is appropriate when someone has already become a customer, making it more likely that they'll purchase again. As you'll learn in chapter 7, repeat customers always spend more, and anything you do to strengthen that relationship goes a long way.

Gifting my clients with note cards created a way for them to easily share my art and generate referrals. (My information is printed on the back side of the folded note card.) This "social sharing" all happened long before social media came along, but I still recommend that my artist clients use physical marketing pieces to promote their art. A social media post slides by in the blink of an eye, but a physical piece will sit on someone's kitchen counter for days (or weeks, if your counter looks anything like mine).

These old-fashioned marketing tactics I learned all those years ago form the foundation of what I use today to sell art and fill my art classes. I've even used physical mail to sell online classes. Of course, digital methods are easier to scale, but there's no spam filter for the postal service, which is why physical mail is so effective. Sending emails and snail mail is part of every successful artpreneur's promotion plan. However, promotion is only one business element you'll need to have in place. To make it as an artpreneur, you'll need to develop all five of the foundations in the Passion-to-Profit framework.

PASSION-TO-PROFIT FRAMEWORK

As mentioned in chapter 1, the Passion-to-Profit framework consists of the five foundations of any sustainable business (whether the business is selling sneakers, jewelry, gym memberships, or paintings). These foundations are production, pricing, prospecting, promotion, and productivity. You'll need to develop skills in each area, and these skills will often overlap and support each other. But a problem or lack of planning in any one foundational area will hinder your success in another.

PRODUCTION

Every business on the planet needs products to sell. Your production plan includes what you plan to sell and how long it takes you to create your products or deliver your service. A solid production plan requires consistently building a profitable body of work and making sure you're producing enough marketable art or offering classes on a steady basis. Artpreneurs understand that they cannot wait for inspiration to strike. Classic mistakes in production include creating art that isn't profitable because the product can't be priced high enough (wrong product, or wrong audience); a lack of capacity to create the products fast enough; and trying to produce too many kinds of products, which makes the artist look like a dabbler rather than a serious professional.

When it comes to building a sustainable income, your production plan goes hand in hand with your pricing plan. In other words, if I were to go into your studio right now and buy everything you've created, would the grand total be the income you're looking for? If you were fully booked, would you have the income you want? For many people, when they do this math, they discover they can't produce fast enough to create the results they desire.

Why No One Wants Your Hand-Painted Rock

FROM: Jane Smith
DATE: February 23, 2021
SUBJECT: help!

Here's the thing, I don't paint on canvas. I paint on rocks.
So, my audience is somewhat limited. Most folks admire
my work, but don't consider it "real art." I can't find the
right venue to sell it. Any ideas? —Jane

Jane believed if only she could find the "right venue" for her rocks, she would have more sales. Sadly, I get emails like this all the time. Whether artists paint onesies, rocks, or mugs, make cute stickers, or crochet doilies, they all want to know how to find an audience for the thing they make, and how to sell said thing. The problem is that they're asking the wrong questions. Instead of asking, "How do I sell this thing?" a better question is, "What sells, and *why*?"

When you're trying to build a sustainable business, focusing on low-cost products is always a mistake. If you're selling inexpensive art, such as hand-painted rocks, stickers, or greeting cards, your profit margin will be low, and you'll struggle to sell enough of them to build a sustainable business. This is always a production problem. Either the art takes too long to produce, relative to what the market commands, or there's an upper limit for the price of the product. The problem isn't the price, but the product. For example, if you want to sell hand-knit sweaters, and each one takes you a full month to complete, it won't be a sustainable business, since few people are likely to spend, say, $5,000 per sweater. If your capacity to create inventory is limited, then the product must command a premium price. Moreover, in most retail businesses you won't sell out everything you create, so your production will have to accommodate creating excess product.

If you're trying to sell too many kinds of things, you'll lack a cohesive marketing message. Many artists enjoy making a variety of things—paintings, sculpture, crafts—but when you offer multiple types of products, you risk turning your small business into a Target, rather than a Tiffany. Target has a sustainable business model because of the volume of products, but most solopreneurs, like us artpreneurs, can't sustain a business based on a variety of low-cost goods. One of the keys to being an artpreneur is understanding that the path to a thriving career requires focusing on the one thing that you do better than anyone else.

Your Capacity to Produce

As you've seen, your production and pricing plans need to work in conjunction with each other. When your capacity to produce your assets is limited, you might have a production problem. Sometimes a production problem can be alleviated simply by raising your prices. My client Linda Doucette complained that she was consistently selling out and couldn't keep up with the gallery orders for her felted and embroidered art. For her, the quick fix was to raise prices immediately. (You'll learn how Linda learned to consistently sell out in chapter 7.) But not all kinds of art command high prices. And if at a low price you can't sell enough pieces to make a living, you'll be better off producing more profitable art. Breaking things down in this manner, many artists have the "aha" moment when they realize: "I can't make a living selling five-dollar greeting cards because I'd have to sell ten thousand of them every year." (And, in fact, given the overhead and cost of producing the cards, the number you'd need to sell is much higher.) Make sure you're creating both consistently and fast enough, and that you're producing art that can be priced at a level high enough to net you sufficient income.

Keep in mind that even if your item is priced at an amount much higher than five dollars, if your profit on the item is only five dollars, then it's still a production problem. I see this happen to a lot of artists who sell their art printed on products. Believing it's easier to sell their art in a form that's useful, they ignore that their profit margins are so low that they must do incredible volume to make the numbers work. Trying to compensate for low-profit art with volume becomes too much of an obstacle. If you've ever said to yourself, "Well, if only I could find a bigger audience, that would solve my problem," you probably have a production problem.

It's much easier to change what you're producing. If the math doesn't work, you're probably producing the wrong thing.

Price × Items Sold Per Year = Gross Income

PRODUCT	QUANTITY SOLD	INCOME
$5 greeting card; e-book	10,000	$50,000
$50 print; scarf	1,000	$50,000
$500 online class; statement necklace; designer pillow	100	$50,000
$2,000 commissioned portrait; family photo shoot	25	$50,000
$5,000 large-canvas art; custom furnishings; bridal gown	10	$50,000

+ + + PIVOT TO PROFITS + + +

Ciara Gilmore had a production problem. She spread herself thin and was a one-stop shop for a hodgepodge of creativity—creating textiles, illustrations, fiber art, and landscape painting. No matter what the request, if a customer wanted something, she felt compelled to make it for them. However, she struggled to connect with collectors and develop a fan base. Customers were confused about her offerings. When she decided to focus on one thing and go all-in on a high-end product, everything changed.

Instead of creating small crafts that customers put on their shelves, Ciara began focusing on abstract art. Now she makes £2,000 per painting, and none of them take much longer to create than the small crafts she used to do. Her customers recognize her value and her profits have soared.

It's not only painters of traditional wall art or "fine artists" who can command high prices. French husband-and-wife artists François-Xavier and Claude Lalanne created soft animal sculptures and artful furniture for over four decades, and their legacy lives on through their influence on other artists. For example, The City Farm Girl (CFG) studio creates felted chicken-shaped footstools inspired by the Lalannes. Their soft sculptures start at $1,650, and they have similar chicken sculptures priced well over $3,650. (Of course, these prices are nothing compared with François-Xavier's sheep-shaped chairs, which fetch multiple six figures at auction.) Since the CFG artists developed a signature style of art that stands out in the marketplace, and positioned these pieces as limited-edition collectibles, they can command high prices in a similar fashion. Understanding how to embrace what makes you special—or even weird—will help you make it as an artpreneur who won't have to compete on price.

THOUGHT WORK

STARVING ARTISTS THINK	ARTPRENEURS BELIEVE
X I just have to sell more.	✔ When I sell art for higher prices, I get to spend more time creating and less time selling, which makes more money.

PRICING

When an artist has a pricing problem, it's not that they *couldn't* command higher prices for their art—it's that they *won't* because mind drama gets in their way. They imagine that collectors are motivated by lower prices, and that they will sell more at lower prices—but that's almost never the case! When my client Kim tried to back out of the landscape commission, it wasn't because my price was too high. She questioned the value of the gift because my price was too low! She started doubting whether giving a landscape to her husband was good enough, or if a *more expensive* set of golf clubs would be a better present . As many people do, she equated a higher price tag with greater value. Had I confidently charged her double for the landscape (as well as taken a deposit from the get-go), she wouldn't have second-guessed her choice.

Why It's So Damned Hard to Raise Your Prices

Even if you understand what's going through your customer's mind as they make a purchase decision, you still might find it difficult to raise your prices. In this case, pricing drama could be getting in your way. Although you may have a myriad of mindset issues around money, here are three reasons you may feel it's difficult to raise your prices.

Reason #1: You're not investing in yourself. If you don't regularly invest in yourself and your business, you'll have trouble setting higher prices. And if you don't believe there are customers out there willing to pay higher prices, it may be because you can't imagine spending that kind of money yourself.

Once I began investing in myself and my business regularly, I learned two useful things. First, when it became normal for me to invest in myself, I no longer had a problem asking others to invest more in themselves. Second, investing in myself reaffirmed my own value and self-worth (like the old saying about how you need to love yourself before looking for love from someone else). Notice ways that you might be scrimping on yourself and your business. For example, artists have asked me whether it was worth spending thirty-five dollars a month on a website. Having a website that makes it easy for people to buy from you is always worth it. If you hope to create a sustainable business, you can't be penny-wise and pound-foolish.

Reason #2: You've internalized sexism and/or racism. If your brain senses that asking for higher prices is risky, it will invent stories about why it's a bad idea. For women, and particularly women of color, or people in marginalized groups, our socialization, parenting, and intergenerational trauma have taught us it isn't proper to make noise, take up space, or be ambitious. Charging higher prices for your art is one of the many ways you can start taking back that power.

Andrea Owen, the author of *Make Some Noise*, explained, "You can take up space with your body, your voice, your power, and confidence. The reason that we don't do this is because we've been conditioned and socialized not to do so—that we're more valued and accepted and loved if we're a 'good girl or a good woman or a good mother': polite, accommodating, putting everyone else's comfort before our own, selfless. I'm not saying that those are bad things. They're great things, but sometimes come at the cost of our own success."[3]

I've noticed that confidence about raising prices has been more difficult for some of my Black clients. To better understand this phenomenon, I invited diversity, equity, and inclusion expert Erica Courdae to discuss "poverty mindset" on my podcast. She shared, "[I'm] literally trying to charge an amount that [my] ancestors were bought and sold for."[4] These clients may not always be aware of the source of their own conditioning and may attribute their reluctance to raise prices to thought distortions (which they may perceive as facts). In addition, when women and people of color look around and see *evidence* of salary discrepancies between genders and races, they're receiving messages from society that they're monetarily worth less! Women's pay in 2022 still lags men's by an average of 10 percent across all industries in the US.[5] For Black women, that pay gap is even wider; the 2020 US Census showed that Black women earned 63 percent of their non-Hispanic White male counterparts.[6] So, if you're part of this demographic, in addition to overcoming your thought distortions, there's an uphill battle to overcome the external ongoing influence of racial oppression.

Reason #3: You're not ready to receive. Using higher prices is one thing but being able to receive the abundance is another. During her interview, Courdae pointed out: "I think the worthiness is a big part of it when there's this subliminal and sometimes very overt conditioning that you're not worthy of this. You're not entitled to this. You don't deserve this." This is tough conditioning to overcome, but it can be done—as we saw with my client Faye, whose art career took off once she was able to shake off the mantle of unworthiness. Recognizing that your thoughts are a product of your conditioning is the first step. Understanding that your thoughts are not *facts* is the next. Not everything we think (or that others think of us) is the truth.

Low-Profit Thinking

Most people are so married to the sabotaging stories they tell themselves that they can't recognize these thought patterns as low-profit thinking. They assume their low-profit thoughts are facts.

Here are some common thought distortions about pricing that will sabotage your results, and replacement thoughts that will help you overcome your own pricing drama.

THOUGHT WORK

STARVING ARTISTS THINK	ARTPRENEURS BELIEVE
X I'm just starting out.	✓ This is just the beginning.
X No one is buying art right now.	✓ Art makes people feel good.
X I can't charge my friends/coworkers/family.	✓ People value what they pay for.
X Online learning is less valuable than in-person learning.	✓ Asynchronous online learning allows students to dive deeper at their own pace.
X Cheaper is easier to sell.	✓ Price isn't always the deciding factor.

PROSPECTING

Prospecting is critical to making it as an artist, and it's the first step in the sales process. Artpreneurs know that they need to find people who love their art and then create a plan to contact these "prospects" in the future. The mistake most artists make is that they meet prospects but don't create a reliable way to stay in touch and ultimately close the sale. Instead, either they hand them a business card or hope their prospects will seek them out on social media.

Artists who focus solely on building a social media following without a reliable way to stay in touch, such as adding them to their email list, will fail to make consistent revenue from their audience. Social media accounts are shut down all the time, with thousands of followers (and all associated online content) vanishing in the blink of an eye. Don't think it can't happen to you because you "follow the rules." My Instagram account got hacked, and it took me over a month to convince Instagram that I was the true owner of the account. One of my clients had her Instagram account shut down without explanation after she posted an artwork of a bird. There's no reliable help desk for this behemoth of a company, and she was left scratching her head wondering what happened and why. Even well-known influencers with hundreds of thousands of followers have seen their accounts get shut down or hacked.

Since these social media firms are private companies, they dictate the terms and can take away your account at any time. They can also choose to end their business or may be subject to the whims of government regulation. Many of us got a taste of a world without the Zuckerverse when all of Meta's apps (including Facebook, WhatsApp, and Instagram) went dark for over six hours on October 4, 2021.

The key to making money with your prospecting efforts is to continually move prospects to your email and contact lists. You can use your email list to send messages in bulk through an email service provider. For that, you must have the person's permission to add them to your email list and include a means for them to unsubscribe. You can also maintain a contact list for sending physical mail or personal one-on-one email. Make sure you consistently get your art and yourself in front of people so that you can find those who want your art and then ask them to take the first step with you by joining your mailing list.

Compiling these lists generally involves getting in front of real human beings so you can communicate with them. Now, of course, you can simulate this process online, but it can be a lot easier and more profitable to learn how to do it in person first. When you start out, you may not be sure exactly what to say or how to say it. Telling everyone you're an artist is a great way to fine-tune your message. Once you master doing it in person, it becomes much easier to move that experience and skill to the online world.

How to Find Prospects

The moment artists realize they need to raise their prices, doubts about where to find buyers willing to pay those higher prices creep in. Belief in your buyer (the customer) is perhaps the most difficult part of the belief triad. Buyers *are* out there—waiting for you to have the confidence to show up and claim your value—but other than thinking positively, exactly how do you *find* them?

There are only three ways to find customers: your platform, other people's platforms, and rented platforms.

Your platform	Your universe, anywhere and everywhere you interact with other humans. This can be online or in person. Your universe will include your social media and content platforms, such as a blog, podcast, or YouTube channel, as well as your in-person experiences.
Other people's platforms	Get attention in other people's universes through introductions, referrals, mentions on other people's blogs, and, of course, press. Press and publicity are by far the best way to build your audience (usually for free) and get your art and services in front of your dreamboat customers.

	Paid advertising can be tricky if you don't have a clearly defined customer avatar. Some artists can do well with paid advertising, such as when your art has a clearly defined customer seeking your kind of art. For example, pet portrait artists can use ads that target pet owners. But for more subjective forms of art, paid advertising may not be the best way to build an audience. For teachers with students actively looking for their type of service, paid advertising is perfect.
Rented platforms (paid advertising)	

In each of the places where you interact with prospects, they'll need a reason to join your email list. Examples of incentives could be a free instructional class, a discount on a purchase, or (my favorite) first dibs on your one-of-a-kind creations.

In April 2022, with the heartbreaking war raging in Ukraine, there was a surge in demand for Ukrainian-style decorated eggs, otherwise known as *pysanky*. The eggs by artist Adriana Wrzesniewski regularly sell out, starting at $40, and many black-and-white designs sell out at $240. Collectors would be happy to join her list to be notified as soon as they're back in stock.

A word of warning. I see too many artists and entrepreneurs rush to scale. They invest in paid advertising methods before they've nailed how to communicate the value they bring to the world. Advertising, including online advertising, can be expensive, and it takes time before it becomes profitable. Even experienced marketers often lose thousands of dollars on advertising that doesn't convert into sales. Until you're ready to gamble on a bigger ad budget, stick to the organic methods described here.

For many artists ready to pay for advertising, a large budget isn't necessary. For example, my client, wildlife artist Elizabeth Mordensky, took out a small series of ads for $750 in an art collector magazine and negotiated a multi-page feature article. As a result of this investment, she sold $9,500 in original artwork.

THOUGHT WORK

STARVING ARTISTS THINK	ARTPRENEURS BELIEVE
✗ All I need to do is make great art.	✓ It's not enough to be awesome. I have to make my own opportunities by building an audience.

PROMOTION

Your promotion plan includes your sales and marketing plans. Many business owners confuse marketing and sales because they both involve forms of promotion, but here's how they differ. Marketing promotions will get the attention of your prospects and convert them into email subscribers. Sales promotion is what you're doing when you talk with someone who has some awareness of you and may be ready to buy. Sales promotions include words on your website and what you say in emails (or in person) to close the sale. For example, many retailers run an annual Black Friday promotion after Thanksgiving. An effective promotion campaign will include a series of emails announcing there will be a sale to drum up anticipation, followed by emails that include a call to action to buy something.

Your promotions should follow this structure. First, whisper that an event is coming, like a new collection drop. Tease that people need to get on your email list so they don't miss out on something special, like an early-bird discount, first dibs, or a limited supply. Then, increase the volume once you've announced the date of your launch, when tickets go on sale, or when your collection drops. Finally, pump up the volume when the event is here—and everyone should buy *now*. You'll notice that this is how live concerts and movies are promoted. You'll see "coming attractions" for movies six months in advance. This promotion builds awareness. Then, once tickets go on sale, the second phase of promotion is selling.

People buy with their emotions, and drumming up desire with a long runway ultimately generates more sales because using a promotional sequence builds anticipation. Many artists use this strategy of an anticipated release date (also known as a "drop" date) to sell collections or mini collections. Part of the thrill for the customers is knowing that the collection may sell out very quickly on opening day, and the fear of missing out motivates them to make a quick decision to buy as soon as the collection is released. This drop strategy has been used across many disciplines including ceramicists, makeup artists, painters, and independent clothing designers.

Ella Emhoff, Vice President Kamala Harris's stepdaughter, released a mini collection of only five knit pieces on the online shopping platform Mall. The heavily promoted collection launch sold out within thirty minutes.[7] But this strategy isn't reserved for influencers or those with famous stepmoms. According to the *New York Times*, Lalese Stamps, a ceramic designer in Columbus, Ohio, regularly sells 250 mugs in under a minute using the "drop" strategy—which essentially involves building anticipation with teasers and then establishing a release date when the entire collection will become available. She's not an anomaly. Brooklyn ceramicist Sarah Hussaini also described selling 350 pieces in six minutes.[8] The coronavirus pandemic fueled a craving for handmade items, especially those that enhanced stay-at-home activities such as curling up in pajamas with a morning cup of coffee in a ceramic mug rather than a Styrofoam cup. These artists (and many others) used the powerful approach of combining an urgency-based selling model with the emotional appeal of handmade crafts during this hands-off time.

THOUGHT WORK

STARVING ARTISTS THINK	ARTPRENEURS BELIEVE
X I need more social media followers.	✔ The better I get at selling, the fewer people I'll need.

PRODUCTIVITY

Once you know all the steps of prospecting and promoting, how do you organize this so you can focus and stop spinning? Technology does help us become more productive through automation, but that's usually only a small piece of the puzzle. Your productivity plan will include all the steps you take from the time you meet a prospect until they finally buy from you—and all the steps in between. Your productivity plan is how you organize yourself to manage your priorities, protect your sacred studio time, and stay focused on your goals. To make it as an artpreneur, you need to become a ninja about managing your priorities and how you spend your days.

My secret to getting so much done while maintaining a life-work balance is using both a digital and an analog calendar to plan my time and manage what I'm doing each day. This keeps my activities focused on my goals rather than just staying busy or spinning. Artist Jeanne Oliver, who homeschooled three children while building her creative business, uses a similar time management system. She says, "People always ask, 'How do you do all of those things?' And it's because I make a plan for it. I figure out, what day am I going to get it done? And I show up on days that I don't feel like showing up."⁹ She shared with me: "I'm not the best teacher, the best businesswoman, or the best artist. It's showing up in little ways consistently." Show up consistently for your art and your business, and you'll make consistent progress as well.

THOUGHT WORK

STARVING ARTISTS THINK	ARTPRENEURS BELIEVE
X I don't have enough time.	✓ When I do what matters most, I get more done in less time.

ARTIST AILMENTS

The three most common ailments plaguing artists are spending time producing low-profit art, low-profit thinking and Rapunzel style marketing. Here's how to self-diagnose each of these and the prescription to fix them.

+ + + DIAGNOSIS + + +

Production Problem:
Spending Too Much Time on Low-Profit Art

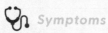 *Symptoms*

1. You're limited by your capacity to create your art.
2. Your art is low profit because it can't be priced higher (items like stickers or greeting cards).
3. You're a jack-of-all-trades, offering too many types of products and services. Both Target and Tiffany sell jewelry, but only Tiffany commands a premium because that store specializes in high-end jewelry and an elite atmosphere.

Focus on creating high-value art with your own signature style.

＋ ＋ ＋ DIAGNOSIS ＋ ＋ ＋

Pricing Problem: Low-Profit Thinking

 *Symptoms*

Low-profit thinking shows up in any of these types of thoughts:

- "No one buys art in my town at those prices."
- "I'm just starting out."
- "I can't charge my friends/coworkers/family."
- "No one is buying art right now. There's a _____ (recession/pandemic/tsunami/etc.)."
- "No one buys art in the summer."
- "It's less valuable if it's online."

 *Prescription*

Start charging premium market value for your art. More important, know and believe in your true worth. Remember, those unhelpful thought distortions demotivate you and sabotage your results.

Starving artists sometimes fall prey to relying on "Rapunzel-style" marketing. In the fairy tale, Rapunzel never leaves her castle and is rescued by a prince who finds her. If you've heard stories of artists being discovered and hope that will happen to you, then you're wishing for a fairy-tale ending. What you might not understand is that the media likes to portray artists as being "discovered," but more often than not, these artists have been working at making their own opportunities for years before the world took notice. Make your own fairy-tale endings through your inspired actions.

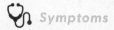

＋ ＋ ＋ DIAGNOSIS ＋ ＋ ＋

Prospecting Problem:
"Rapunzel-Style" Marketing

 Symptoms

1. You hope customers will contact you from your posts on Instagram.
2. You hand out business cards, imagining prospects will follow up.
3. You believe your followers see everything you post. (Spoiler alert: Fewer than 1 percent of your posts appear in the Instagram newsfeed of any one follower.)
4. You hide behind the punch bowl at your art openings.

Prescription

1. Actively build an email list so you can contact prospects without relying on the fickleness of an algorithm.
2. Pitch stories to local news outlets about your art and events.

MARKETING MALPRACTICE

In many cases, artists misdiagnose the problems that limit them. You may think your problem is in one area, say prospecting, when really it's in another, like pricing. Think you need a bigger audience? Maybe you're too focused on low-profit art (a production problem), or maybe you're pricing your existing art too low (a pricing problem). Think you don't know how to sell on social media? Typically, that means you aren't using social media to *connect* and *prospect* (a prospecting problem), or you don't know how to close sales (a promotion problem). Think you don't have time to get it all done? When you've misdiagnosed your problem, you're spending time on the wrong things (a productivity problem). Generally, these classic mistakes occur when an artist doesn't understand the five foundations of building a business or because of limiting beliefs that inevitably affect their progress.

MISDIAGNOSIS	ACTUAL PROBLEMS
X "I just need a bigger audience."	✓ You're focused on low-profit art (production). ✓ You're not pricing your art high enough (pricing). ✓ You don't know how to promote to your existing audience (promotion).
X "I don't know how to sell on social media."	✓ You're not using social media to build a connection with them. ✓ You're not building your email list (prospecting) or using your email list to sell (promotion).
X "I don't have enough time to do it all."	✓ You're spending too much time on the wrong tasks (productivity). ✓ You're producing art that takes too long to create (production). ✓ You're not pricing your art high enough (pricing).

	✓ You're trying to make up the low prices with high volume.
✗ "I don't have enough time to do it all."	✓ You lack a solid foundation on how to promote and prospect, so you spend your time creating content for the Zuckerverse instead of doing what matters most (prospecting and promotion).

Have you noticed what all these problems have in common? Focusing on the wrong things! When you're doing the wrong things, you'll spend a lot of time spinning and frustrated. You'll be working hard but not making progress. Let's review what you need to focus on, so you gain forward momentum.

PASSION-TO-PROFIT FRAMEWORK

- **Production Plan:** Consistently build a body of work and commit to your sacred creative time.
- **Pricing Plan:** Your prices and the amount of production you create with your production plan must add up to the income you're seeking. If not, you'll need to raise your prices (or revisit the production plan to readjust offerings).
- **Prospecting Plan:** Build a list of people who are prepared to pay top dollar. Building a list of collectors who love you and your art is easier than you think (without using expensive advertising).
- **Promotion Plan:** Turn prospects into repeat buyers and raving fans. Learn what to say so your ideal buyers joyfully whip out their credit cards to purchase your art.
- **Productivity Plan:** Get the right things done (with more focus) in less time.

WHAT ARTPRENEURS NEED TO BELIEVE

- Traditional sales techniques can be used to sell anything, including art.
- Pricing your art and services for profit is just math.
- Buyers are out there waiting for you to have the confidence to show up and demonstrate your value.

MARCHING ORDERS

- If you were fully booked or sold out of your inventory, would that give you the income you're seeking? If not, you need to create more, change what you're producing, and/or raise your prices!
- Pitch stories to local news outlets about your art and events to garner free publicity.
- Use your social media in addition to in-person events and publicity to find new prospects.
- Actively build an email list so you can contact prospects without relying on the fickleness of an algorithm. (We'll talk more about building an email list in chapter 8.)

NEXT STEPS

Over the next five chapters, we'll explore each of the five parts of the Passion-to-Profit framework (beginning with production) so that you'll understand how to apply them. If you want to make a sustainable living as an artpreneur, you'll need to produce art that's marketable. But what makes art marketable? That's what we're covering next.

"ART DOES NOT EXIST ONLY TO ENTERTAIN, BUT ALSO TO CHALLENGE ONE TO THINK, TO PROVOKE, EVEN TO DISTURB, IN A CONSTANT SEARCH FOR THE TRUTH."

—BARBRA STREISAND

EMBRACE YOUR INNER WEIRDO

WHEN MY FOURTH-GRADE TEACHER DUBBED me "class artist," I transformed my internal self-concept from "weird new girl" to "artist." All those traits that I thought had made me weird or different were actually my superpowers that enabled me to see differently and hence make art. To be an artist is to identify connections in the world and help people see the world in a different way. That's what art does. When you create art (and your marketing), you'll also learn to embrace your inner weirdo so that your art stands out.

In the last chapter, you read about the five foundations of the Passion-to-Profit framework for building your business—including production. One of the keys to creating a solid production plan is creating marketable art. But what makes art marketable?

• • •

HOW TO CREATE YOUR OWN SIGNATURE BRAND

Your audience is looking for something different from what's already out there. They're tired of the same old, same old. That's why a marketable production plan includes developing a signature style and brand. Since you can't separate the art from the artist, your signature brand will include the kind of art you produce, your messaging, and the way you show up in the world. Jennifer Kem, a brand-building and leadership expert in the Bay Area who works with celebrity businesses such as the Oprah Winfrey Network, defines brand this way: "Your brand is the soul of how you're communicating, how you help people, and what experience they can expect to have in the world. The brand is your art and the rest is science. Marketing is a science. Sales is a science. But your brand is the soul of how you're presenting yourself in the world in all forms."[1] Without a signature brand and style, you'll struggle to market effectively because your body of work won't be cohesive.

Regardless of the marketplace in which you're selling—online or in-person—or the art form, all the artist's work should feel like it's made by the same artist. Stylistic choices matter in all art forms. If you're a choreographer, is your style modern, classical, or some hybrid? Musicians might be drawn to atonal patterns, as in the work of Schoenberg, or to more Romantic motifs, like those pioneered in the works of Clara Schumann. As you experiment, your signature style may evolve over time, but should consistently reflect who you are at any given moment.

The art you create will be an extension of your brand's message, and vice versa. Your brand and signature style go hand in hand. Many new business owners believe their brand is limited to the colors, fonts, and logo that appear on their website. However, India Jackson, founder of the brand and visibility agency Flaunt Your Fire, offered a broader definition, sharing: "When we think of branding, we think of it as your public image, your reputation. The colors, the logo, the type of art that you create, how you dress, what your photographs look like, what your captions are about, what subjects you cover when you are connecting with your people. These are all shaping what would be said about you, but they're not necessarily the brand on their own."[2] In other words, anything you do and say will be perceived as part of your brand—especially as an artist, since we are considered "personal brands." That's why we'll be talking about your overall message as part of your signature style.

Developing a signature style and brand requires vulnerability because your values, quirks, and imperfections inform your distinctive voice. As you make your voice more apparent, these differences will likely attract both fans and haters. Avoid the temptation to play down your uniqueness to appease the haters. Playing a more audacious game always attracts haters because they resent you showing up in the world in a way that they're still afraid to do. Some people will find fault with you no matter what you do; but if they hate you for your uniqueness, at least you'll know you're doing something right. And please resist the urge to keep your art and style under wraps as it evolves just to avoid negative feedback. Business coach Jason Van Orden agrees: "Your voice is the thing that only you can bring to the world, but it takes some time to really embody it to a level that people have no choice but to take notice."[3] So go out and start expressing your voice as you're discovering and developing your signature style.

All nine of these following steps ask you to be authentic and vulnerable, and to lean into everything that makes you unique.

Step One: Go Beyond Your Influences

Once you've mastered the fundamentals of your art, you'll be more comfortable breaking the rules to add your own spin to what you've learned. Don't make the mistake that many novices make of looking around to see what's selling and try to imitate that. Too many artists have no idea how to create something original to stand out in a crowded marketplace. I've also noticed a race to emulate what's popular in the way new business owners operate. For example, they've learned how to imitate the mannerisms of the gurus they admire, but they lack originality in developing their own marketing voice. In the bro-marketing world, goateed Tony Robbins minions with their matching black turtlenecks jockey for attention, while in the spiritual guru space, long-haired Gabby Bernstein wannabes sip coffee with nut milk.

There's nothing wrong with modeling successful people—at first. In fact, learning from the masters is a crucial step in your journey to becoming great yourself. Even the most acclaimed painters and sculptors of all time also learned through copying. Degas copied Rembrandt. Michelangelo studied Greek sculpture to better pose the body in marble. However, Degas eventually embraced a style that looked nothing like Rembrandt, and although Michelangelo's sculpting skills rivaled the Greeks, you'd never confuse one of his sculptures with one done by Rodin or Camille Claudel.[4]

Many artists develop a marketable style by taking existing ideas and putting their own spin on them. For example, Picasso was infamous for taking somebody else's idea and then executing it ten times better. But Picasso never copied *popular* trends. He adapted unpopular avant-garde ideas and then made them popular by adding that little twist so that, suddenly, people understood the new art form. Overall, the key to creating a signature style and brand is to sprinkle a bit of spice from each of your influences and combine them in a new way so you're completely original.

When my students ask, "How do I create my own style?" I tell them, "It's not about creating a style. It's about *uncovering* what's already there, buried deep inside." When you take off the training wheels and stop depending on copying others, your unique style will appear. Everyone already has a style of their own; they just don't know what it is yet. What makes uncovering one's style so difficult is that most of us, women especially, have put ourselves on the back burner for our entire lives, which means we've never spent any time uncovering any parts of ourselves, let alone our own artistic styles.

Creating and marketing your art should be a joyful process. When you start exploring and discovering what you love about that process, you'll be making artistic choices that enhance that joy. For example, if you're a visual artist, you may be drawn to certain colors because of how they make you feel; or you'll start to have fun with wonky lines because you get impatient with precise details; or you'll realize you want to put polka dots on everything because you like them. Japanese artist Yayoi Kusama began creating intricate polka-dot art almost obsessively. Kusama has been very open about her lifelong struggle with mental illness and credits her art with giving her an outlet for her obsessiveness. She first emerged on the avant-garde scene in 1968,[5] and her art has gone in and out of fashion. Now well into her nineties, her polka-dot sculptural installations attract millions in the most prestigious venues around the world.

Finding your own style is like the process we all went through as adolescents, trying to navigate fashion trends. (Now, I know some of you might be shaking your heads because you *still* don't have your own fashion style. I get that.) But if your style is based on copying others, you'll never feel as though you've done it right. For example, no matter what I wore to my kids' school events, I couldn't capture the "expensive yet casual" look those other moms nailed so effortlessly. Now that I'm in my fifties, it's a different story because the truth is I really don't care anymore (not to mention that PTA events are ancient history). I'm done copying other people's styles and calling them my own. If I feel comfortable wearing it, then it's the perfect thing to wear. I don't need to wear a uniform or look like the people around me. And I'm *happy* to look different. I want to be weird in my dress, art, and business. When I create, I want to go to a place that's unusual, embrace my inner weirdo, and trust my intuition. Eccentricities make art better, more memorable, and ultimately more marketable.

Step Two: Amplify Your Quirks

You can develop your authentic voice by embracing what makes you weird. Although the word "weird" might make you feel uncomfortable or may sound insulting, consider the origin of the word. The history of the word "weird" can be traced to Scotland and was popularized in Shakespeare's *Macbeth*. The weird sisters prophesize Macbeth's destiny, and in Elizabethan England, the word "weird" meant "fate" or "destiny." The association with the supernatural morphed the word's overall meaning. As people began to reject the mystical and supernatural, "weird" began to take on negative connotations. But where your art is concerned, remember the word's origin.

Society trains us to vilify anything that's eccentric or different. When we recognize traits of our own artistic voice that differ from the mainstream, we need to deliberately raise our authentic voices, not quiet them. To make it as an artpreneur, amplify the very things you might consider weird about you and your art. At its core, weirdness is the magic that separates the merely mundane from the truly special. And embracing that magic is the secret to fulfilling your destiny as an artist.

Make sure your marketing reflects your quirks as well. One of my former business coaches, Ron Reich,[6] likes to call himself a "quirky marketing genius." He encourages entrepreneurs to lean into their quirks and talk about them because these are the things "that make you more of a multidimensional person." His advice is to ask yourself, "What are one or two things about you that have nothing to do with your expertise or being an artist, but just are interesting, that people are going to relate to?" When Reich shows up on social media, writes emails, or is interviewed on podcasts, he talks about his dog, Trevor, his obsession with Nutella, and fitness. He recognizes what he's doing. "We got a little bit of a juxtaposition there, which is it's more interesting that I'm a fitness dude who's into Nutella."

When you're lost for words in your marketing, think about obsessions of your own that have nothing to do with your art, and talk about them. Your audience wants to connect with the real you behind the creations. They may not share the same obsessions, but those idiosyncrasies make you a more relatable person.

Step Three: Stop People-Pleasing

If you're reluctant to be weird, or even different, it may be because you're inclined to people-please. People-pleasers create art that resembles what's most popular, not because they don't know how to create different or original art, but because they're afraid of what other people might think. When I interviewed life coach Shaun Roney,[7] we discussed how people-pleasing sabotages art

people-pleasing

showing up in a way that you think will make people like you better

and business success. She shared that it's a waste of energy to try anticipating what anyone else might think. And, more importantly, she asked, "Are you actually being authentically you?"

When you hide your eccentricities, you're not showing up authentically—and, most often, these are the very things that make you memorable! When you market your art, make your point of view stand out from the crowd. Stop worrying about being weird and pleasing everyone; instead, make and promote that special art that only you can.

Step Four: Share Your Values

Many artists fear that if they reveal their beliefs, they'll alienate people. Believe it or not, this is what you *want* to do. I asked Michael F. Schein, author of *The Hype Handbook* and founder of MicroFame Media, why he encourages his clients to "pick fights." He pointed out that "you can pick a fight with an idea; you can pick a fight with another scene. The abstract expressionists picked a fight with who came before them, and then the pop artists picked a fight with the abstract expressionists."[8]

You can find examples of this in all art forms. For example, the grunge music of the nineties, popularized by rockers like Courtney Love and bands like Nirvana, were rejections of the computer-generated sound of the eighties.

Then the women of the post-grunge musical era, such as Alanis Morissette, wrote and performed songs that defined what it meant to be a woman, that contrasted with Nirvana's aggressively male sexual "cock-rock" in the decade that preceded her. When you present your point of view in a way that contrasts with the artists who came before you, you create a brand that stands out and will be marketable.

One can't talk about what it means to own your voice without highlighting Beyoncé, the queen of R&B and one of the best-selling recording artists of all time. To date, she's been awarded twenty-eight Grammys and sold 118 million records worldwide. Yet her music isn't for everyone, as she stands firmly in her activism. Unafraid of alienating Republicans, Beyoncé has performed in fundraising efforts for both Barack Obama and Hillary Clinton. And at a 2016 Clinton fundraiser, her backup dancers performed in pantsuits and "I'm with her" T-shirts.[9] Moreover, Beyoncé's "Flawless" lyrics sample Nigerian activist and author Chimamanda Ngozi Adichie's TEDx Talk "We Should All Be Feminists."[10] Your values become part of your message, and your brand embodies your signature style and will be perceived as part of your artist persona.

Throughout history, you'll find countless examples of artists who highlighted their values. Late-nineteenth-century France offers a good example. At a time when many people felt defensive, insecure, xenophobic, and nationalistic, a heightened climate of anti-Semitism took hold, and the French government wrongly accused a Jewish captain, Alfred Dreyfus, of treason. Novelist, playwright, and journalist Émile Zola published an editorial piece in support of Dreyfus, putting pressure on the government to reopen the case. Known as the Dreyfus affair, this political scandal divided France into pro-republican, anticlerical Dreyfusards and pro-Army, mostly Catholic anti-Dreyfusards. Records show that Claude Monet, Camille Pissarro, and Marcel Proust were pro-Dreyfus while Cézanne and Degas were both anti-Dreyfus. (Degas was most vocal about his anti-Semitic opinions.) Auguste Renoir hoped to appear "neutral."

As the country was divided, this had far-reaching ripple effects in the French art world. Rodin reneged on a commission sponsored by pro-Dreyfusards.[11] Moreover, Renoir refused to "exhibit with a gang of Jews and Socialists."[12] A whole nation looked to artists and asked them, "Which side are you on?"

Trying to appear neutral on lightning-rod political subjects is a particular form of people-pleasing. You cannot choose both sides of an issue, especially as an artist looking to define your voice. Your opinions, values, and quirks all become part of that. Fast-forward to today, when the United States has been experiencing its own period of great insecurity, xenophobia, anti-Semitism, and nationalism. The murder of George Floyd in May 2020 triggered a social justice movement and a level of civil unrest and positive activism across the globe.

On the weekend following the murder of Floyd, I came across an Instagram video by business coach and author Rachel

Rodgers with the cynical caption, "the good white liberal response." Rodgers appears without makeup or pretense in an unscripted, raw, and emotional rant. She clearly intended it for her audience, but the publicly shared video went viral within hours.

When I finished watching it, I looked up at my husband and sighed. "I screwed up."

My husband lifted his eyes from his crossword puzzle. "What are you talking about?"

I told him about Rodgers's response to a well-known business coach who had shut down her Facebook group's chat feature because she didn't want to facilitate tough conversations in the wake of George Floyd's death.

"Yeah, that's terrible," he agreed, "but I still don't understand what this has to do with you."

"It's about White privilege," I said weakly. "*I'm* part of that problem."

As an art teacher, I hold space for students of all beliefs. Up to that point, I had thought sharing my beliefs on my public social media platforms would repel those who voted differently than I. (It does!) However, since I hadn't been forthright about sharing my own values publicly, no one knew what they were. As a result, I hadn't attracted an audience in alignment with my values either. In addition, I also hadn't made enough of an effort to invite people to my podcast who reflected the art world's broad diversity. Although I consistently highlighted female artists and thought leaders, I hadn't done enough to be inclusive of all women. Rodgers's video was more than a critique of any leader when she said, "If it doesn't cost you anything, it's not enough."[13] *I knew I could do better.* Now, my podcast regularly highlights people of all races, religions, and sexual orientations and as a result, the audience that I serve reflects a strong commitment to diversity, equity, and inclusion.

As artists, we respond to our world by creating metaphors that show people how to feel. Politics, the environment, social justice, sex—these are all part of our world. To be an artist is to share your feelings about your ideals through your art, words, and actions. Some of us convey messages directly through art. Others take a stand through public words and actions. And, of course, some do both. But no matter what kind of art you create, your words and actions will become part of your message.

Art is about taking risks. And artpreneurs take risks in all areas of life. They live their art and embody it on all levels to remain true to their beliefs and core values—without looking over their shoulder to see what others think. And they don't make statements just to be performative. When you share your authentic self, not everyone will like you—but if they don't like you, at least let it be for the right reasons. I generally don't consider my art a form of activism. Yet on October 8, 2020, I had an idea. I posted my watercolor painting of a fly on social media with the following caption: "Behold the humble housefly. They are naturally attracted to anything rotten or dying." This one small fly unleashed a maelstrom under the post. Hundreds of people announced their outrage, including this comment: "Done with you. Love art... not politics with my art." On the other hand, others responded in favor of the content. "Never mind the unfollowers. I'll follow you harder."

On any other day, the fly (and my caption) would've gone unnoticed. But this post generated hundreds of shares, comments, and reactions of all sorts because I posted this watercolor one day after the vice-presidential debate. For a few minutes of the debate, a fly had stolen the show by landing on the snow-white hair of Mike Pence. I loved how the simplicity of the post triggered an outsized reaction. Although I lost many followers that day with just one fly, I gained something larger. I showcased a piece of art that made people think. I took a risk, and in doing so, shared my values.

While conducting research for this book, I revisited the post to pull some comments representative of the reaction (without including anyone's personal politics, which are beside the point). A comment I hadn't noticed before made me smile: "This is a beautiful piece. Of course, artists interpret and create art based upon current events. That's what's meant to happen." The commenter? Rachel Rodgers.

Step Five: Embrace Imperfection

Lis Lewis knows a thing or two about what separates the merely talented from those who rise to superstardom. As a celebrity vocal coach, she has worked with rock stars such as Rihanna, Miguel, Demi Lovato, Courtney Love, Britney Spears, and many others. She believes it's personality rather than perfection that makes all the difference. In an interview with *HITS* magazine, she shares, "You don't want them all to sound beautiful; some people shouldn't. Some people have a rasp or some other particular quality, and you don't want to lose that. I like to think I specialize in helping each person bring out who they are."[14] Lewis also notes that superstar Britney Spears set herself apart by injecting "Valley Girl talk" into her singing.[15] When Spears recorded her hits in the late nineties, this vocal style was revolutionary. Since then, there have been so many copycats that we take her innovative approach for granted.

Here's what you need to know. Britney Spears differentiated herself from other singers by leaning into the stylistic quirks that others viewed as mistakes. Had Britney's vocal coach tried to normalize these differences, you might be asking yourself, "Britney who?" Leaning into stylistic variations set her apart, which helped her reach the highest level of attention and stardom. Her differences made her music resonant, compelling, and interesting. Beyond her voice, her personality, look, and overall point of view made her unique, allowing her team to crank the idiosyncrasies all the way up to an 11.

Here's the main thing I want you to remember: you do not have to give up your weirdness to create art. In fact, the exact opposite is true. You must *give in* to your weirdness to create art. Go to that place that's different from everyone else and create art that's different without caring about what other people think. Don't get mad or upset or be resentful. Just embrace that weirdness on every level. The best art in the world is produced by us weirdos. Don't imagine you need to make everything perfect; after all, perfection is an arbitrary construct. Just incorporate your differences, quirks, values, and weirdness into your art. Crank up the volume on all that makes you different!

Step Six: Honor What Comes Easy for You

My husband decided to plant a garden this year. He went to a nursery and picked out pricey baby starter tomato, eggplant, and pepper plants. While he was at the register, he tossed in a few cheap packets of seeds for sunflowers, cucumbers, and green beans. When he got home, I helped him empty the back of our SUV of all the trays. In the hot sun, we dug holes for each of the baby plants. This process took all afternoon. Then, he remembered the seed packets and sprinkled the seeds around the perimeters of the empty beds.

The baby starter plants looked so promising with their leaves blowing in the wind. Unfortunately, within a few weeks, the eggplants we worked so hard to plant shriveled on the vine. We lost most of the tomato crop to hungry insects. Finally, the pepper plants produced a few anemic-looking vegetables but were nothing to write home about. By contrast, within a few weeks, sprouts from the scattered seeds pushed through the soil, and within a month those plants caught up in size to the pricier starter plants. Shortly after that, each of the bean plants dangled jewels of beautiful long string beans, and the cucumber plants were adorned with white flowers. During the hot months of July and August, we had enough cucumbers to feed us and all of our neighbors. Moreover, the sunflowers that started off as humble seeds towered over the garden with their huge van Gogh–sized faces of yellow gold. Next year, we'll be sticking with the ease of the seed packets. Sometimes the things that come easy work out the best.

Society teaches that you must shed blood, sweat, and tears for your work to have value. For artists, as well, when something comes easily to us, we may not value it as much; this of course leads us to underprice our art. For example, when wedding photographers want to switch from backbreaking gigs every week to family portrait sessions that pay twice as much for less work, they might feel guilty. But just because your art form is easy or pleasurable for you doesn't mean it's not valuable. Honor what comes easy to you and remember that just because it's easy for you doesn't mean it's easy for most people. What took you an hour may take someone else all day, or they may not be able to do it at all.

Step Seven: Open Yourself Up to Feedback

Don't wait until you've found your voice before you start marketing yourself. I see too many artists who want to disappear in their studios and not come out until they've perfected a style. They believe that marketing an immature style will hurt their careers—when in fact the exact opposite is true! You won't discover your signature voice in the studio. Go out and perform it. Part of identifying your voice is opening yourself up to feedback, and marketing your art is the best way to do that. You'll need time to identify your uniqueness as your style evolves. You might not even notice what makes you unique, but feedback from your audience will help you recognize your special sauce.

That's why I continue to exhibit in person. Art shows are a lot of work, but the feedback lets me know what my audience is interested in. I also continued to teach in-person even after I got the online art classes going. I understood that the real-time feedback from students made me a better instructor. You'll get some feedback online, but mostly you're either going to get positive feedback or silence. You can't learn anything from silence.

A marketable style doesn't mean everyone loves your art. When you do arrive at your signature style, it will be marketable because, though some will hate it, others will *love* it.

Step Eight: Stop Procrasti-Learning

Another reason artists don't market their style while it's evolving is that they're stuck in procrasti-learning mode. Recognize that procrasti-learning is a form of perfectionism that will sabotage your results. When I interviewed Ronnie Walter, author of *License to Draw*, about licensing art, she shared, "It's easy to hide in the research phase." She said artists often tell her, "Well, I need to know everything about licensing. I need to know everything about contracts. I need to know everything about this," or "I need to have all of this artwork." Walter agreed that feedback is crucial for building a successful commercial portfolio so you can continue to improve your artwork, and she added, "If you wait until the very end, you got a big road ahead if it's not resonating with anyone." Yes, you need to be proficient in your craft before you build a business from it, but you don't need to wait until it's perfect. Artists who wait for everything to be perfect never get a business going.

Step Nine: Love Your Baby Now

I call the reluctance to market a style as it's evolving "Sleeping Beauty Complex." In the Disney version of the Sleeping Beauty fairy tale, a young princess is raised by fairies, who protect her from an evil curse, until she becomes a woman. Artists who have Sleeping Beauty Complex want to hide their art away until it's fully evolved or grown up so that they can avoid criticism or negative feedback. The best way to know if your style is marketable is to start marketing it. Don't wait until your art baby is fully grown before you start loving your art. Love your baby now!

When you're just starting out, you may not have lots of fans to validate an idea, but if at least one person loves your art, you've got something to go on. As money mindset mentor Kelly Hollingsworth likes to say, "Fans are like cockroaches. Where there's one, there's two. Where there's two, there's four. You just must know and trust and believe that there is more there. If one person loved it and if it resonated with one person, it will be true with lots of people."[16]

When you're about to ask people for feedback, revisit the belief triad. Your belief in your art shouldn't depend on what people think. If you ask questions such as, "Do you like it?" or "What do you think of my art?" then you're coming from a place of low confidence. People respond differently to the meek question "What do you think?" than they do to the confident statement "Look at this!" If you ask for feedback from a place of low confidence, it will negatively influence the feedback you receive.

I see this all the time with artists in their emails. You have to say, "This is my yacht," not "I have this leaky rowboat." Stop apologizing! If you ask for feedback in a way that presumes your art is less than, you'll be more likely to get negative feedback. When you communicate confidently, you'll receive better feedback. The more you communicate with confidence, the more easily you'll sell your art (and your ideas), no matter what you're creating. How you feel about yourself, and how you feel about what you're making, will impact your results.

Hollingsworth agrees. She explained, "There's an energy about yourself when you're creating that informs what you create. There's bravery, there's courage. You're doing things that other people won't do. If you're feeling unconfident, that will impair your art and it will impair the way you describe your art to others." In other words, if you're low on the belief scale, your production process will be adversely affected. So, love your baby now!

+ + + **MINDSET CHECK-IN** + + +

What's coming up for you? Write down all your fears about expressing yourself in your art and marketing messages in a way that feels true and authentic. Label your thought distortions.

Mind reading = MR | Fortune-telling = FT
All-or-nothing thinking = AON

Notice which thoughts aren't serving you.

WHAT ARTPRENEURS NEED TO BELIEVE

- Embrace vulnerability every step of the way while developing a signature style and brand.
- Sprinkle just a bit of spice from each of your influences and combine them in a new way so you're completely original.
- At its core, weirdness is the magic that separates the merely mundane from the truly special—and it's the secret to fulfilling your destiny as an artist.

- When your style is based on copying other people, you'll always feel as though you've done it wrong.

MARCHING ORDERS

- Go beyond your influences.
- Amplify your quirks.
- Stop people-pleasing.
- Share your values.
- Embrace imperfection.
- Honor what comes easy for you.
- Open yourself up to feedback.
- Stop procrasti-learning.
- Love your baby now.

"KNOW THAT YOU CAN START LATE, LOOK DIFFERENT, BE UNCERTAIN, AND STILL SUCCEED."

—MISTY COPELAND

THINK LIKE AN
ABUNDANT ARTIST

IN THE EIGHTIES, BEING "COOL" meant you sported an armful of black rubber bracelets; a ripped, shoulder-exposing, neon sweatshirt; and moussed-up hair—an androgynous look popular with men and women. I pulled off this "street urchin" aesthetic with my babysitting earnings. During this era, an alternative version of cool included lots of Gucci and other designer brands, and New York City street vendors preyed on tourists (and girls like me) with their knockoffs. Once, I bought a fake Gucci watch, only to throw it out a few weeks later. Suzie, the Queen Bee who ruled our school, sat behind me in geometry. "Y'know that's a *fake*," she hissed in my ear. She then schooled me on the differences between my obviously fake watch and her real one.

The Suzies of the world look at your low-priced art and wonder, "What's wrong with it?" When painters price their art too low, people often ask, "Is this a print or an original?" Pricing anything too low will lead prospective customers to question both its value and its authenticity. If people aren't buying from you, you might think it's because your prices are too high—but the problem could be that your prices are too low.

We're going to unpack the psychological factors that drive people to pay a premium for goods and services. You'll discover why it's a mistake to focus on low-cost products and why you might be holding yourself back from asking for higher prices because you believe cheaper is easier to sell. (Spoiler alert: It isn't.) Don't worry. I promise to explain why right now.

The coronavirus pandemic, the rise of Amazon, and social justice activism all created dramatic shifts in the way people shop. In 2021, Amazon, with its free shipping and easy from-click-to-front-door service, unseated Walmart as the retail giant.[1] Supply chain issues and inflation further undermined brand loyalty.[2] However, not all buyers are looking for what's cheapest—or even what's most popular. A conscious consumer may care more about a company's alignment with their values. Moreover, buyers hit hard by the doldrums of living through the pandemic are less price-sensitive and tend to choose items that provide fantasy and escape. Good news for those offering either art or art classes.

PRICING DRAMA

As we saw in chapter 5, pricing drama occurs when artists have thought distortions within the belief triad, which include thoughts about yourself, the value of your art, and your customer's willingness to buy your art (at a premium). If you have a belief deficit in any of those three areas, it will drive your prices down. For an artpreneur, this is a recipe for disaster. Your reasons for not charging more may sound good to you, but it's your fear that's driving the bus—and holding you back.

Fear shows up as doubt, and our brains come up with stories about why charging more won't work for us. We evolved with fear as our default setting because our brains are built for survival, not goal achievement. Anytime you're uncomfortable, your brain will conjure multiple reasons why you shouldn't do that unfamiliar, scary thing. And the smarter you are, the better your brain will be at coming up with convincing stories.

ABUNDANT ARTIST LESSONS

To shift your mindset from scarcity to abundance, you first need to start thinking like a buyer. Using real-world examples, I'm going to share fourteen lessons you can use for tapping into buyer psychology that also consider modern shifts in their behavior. This way you'll be fully armed with the latest research to overcome the biggest challenges when pricing and marketing your art while keeping in mind how buyers actually think and respond.

Abundant Artist Lesson #1: Low prices are a turn-off.

A question of taste. My husband, Ron, loves a "good" glass of wine with dinner. Sometimes he lets me choose the bottle (knowing that my preference is based solely on the appeal of the label's artwork) but instructs me to get a "good" bottle, which he defines as costing twenty dollars or more. Ron, who would automatically sail past the twelve-dollar "no good" wines, instructs me to go to the middle shelf. Meanwhile, other wine drinkers probably turn up their noses at our twenty-dollar wine selections and only consider wines priced at forty dollars and up. And so on. I've read arguments that only wine connoisseurs should invest in the premium bottles since the rest of us prefer sweeter wines, which are cheaper.[3] But the point isn't whether more expensive wine tastes better. It's that we assume the higher price translates to higher quality. My husband has never said, "This wine should be more expensive." He just assumes the more expensive wines taste better, and cheaper ones aren't as good.

My husband isn't alone. In a 2015 study, researchers proved that in blind taste tests, samplers enjoyed the wines more when they were told that they were more expensive.[4] Dan Kennedy, in his book *No B.S. Price Strategy*, described this phenomenon as "reassuringly expensive."[5] Art connoisseurs are luxury buyers who expect higher prices to denote value. We see the placebo effect of higher prices increasing enjoyment across a diverse range of products and services, including the arts, and I've experienced this myself. For example, one of my most popular online classes is Watercolor Portrait Academy. When I initially offered this class in 2013, I priced it at $97 and had trouble marketing it. When I bumped the price to $197 just a year later, without making any changes to the content, something interesting happened. My new students, who had paid the higher price, enjoyed the course more. The higher tuition enhanced their perceived value of the course. In addition, since they had paid more, they were more emotionally invested in completing the course. The higher course-completion rate led to more students getting better results. In other words, raising the price created more value for my art students. In 2020, I added more content to the course, with additional demonstrations to make sure students learned how to paint a diversity of flesh tones and hair types, and raised the price further to $497. At this price, I make more money, and because I'm working with fewer students, they receive the added benefit of more personalized attention.

A question of trust. There are probably a number of areas in your life where you're not that price-sensitive. For example, if you've ever had a sick pet, I bet you didn't choose a veterinarian because they were the cheapest. Suppose your vet told you, "Cocoa needs lifesaving surgery, and the fee is $1,000." Would you look for a vet to do it for less? Probably not. You'd probably stay with your vet because you trust their services. (My ten-year-old cat, Ebony, has lived a healthy life, so I'm a bit out of date on vet prices, but I imagine lifesaving surgery must cost much more than $1,000, since we recently paid more than $800 to get her teeth cleaned.)

Artists just starting out tend to think they need to price their art and services low, but other professionals (dentists, lawyers, etc.) don't do this! Sometimes, one's experience can command a higher price. For example, I might be more inclined to pay more for a videographer who has twenty years' experience. However, if I wanted someone to create TikTok videos or Reels, then I wouldn't be looking for someone with that many years under their belt, because those platforms haven't even been around that long. In that case, I might choose a videographer starting out because they may have a youthful style and are more cutting edge. If you're creating art that offers a fresh perspective with a unique, signature style, as we discussed in the last chapter, then it won't matter how long you've been at it.

Abundant Artist Lesson #2: Don't crowdsource prices.

If you price your art based on what others are charging, you're probably underpricing your art. This is because the artists whose prices you emulate likely have pricing drama of their own! To make matters worse, you may be tempted to charge slightly less than the people whose prices you copy because you don't yet know how else to distinguish yourself from the other artists in your medium. To be honest, this is exactly how I priced my first series of portraits. I went online, looked at what other portrait artists were charging, found a local artist who charged $300 for each child's portrait—and since I was just starting out, I priced my first family portraits at $200 per child. (Classic rookie mistake!)

Shortly after I began letting people know I was open for business, my friend Meredith wanted commissioned portraits of her two children. At that time, I worked from my clients' photos rather than taking my own. After an hour of helping her sort through family pictures, she chose three photos of each child she wanted painted. In other words, she was perfectly happy spending $600 for each child. When a client is quick to buy and seems to buy more than they need, it's a red flag indicating that you're under-charging. Based on that, I raised my price to $750 per child, almost four times my original price—and this increase hasn't hurt my sales at all.

When I suggest to clients that they raise their prices, they worry that there are buyers who may have been "thinking about it" with the old price, and for whom the new price will kill the sale. We flatter ourselves by thinking that people remember our old prices and notice the new ones, when in reality we're the only ones paying attention to our pricing.

When I was overwhelmed with pet portrait commissions, I instructed my assistant to double all the prices. She raised them, but within a week I received three new orders at the higher price. One of the orders came from a client who had paid the lower price the prior year. She didn't question the price increase one bit—a sign that my new prices were probably still too low!

Pricing your art by asking everyone in your life what they think your prices should be is known as "crowdsourcing prices." This practice is especially harmful when you're asking others who may have their own limiting beliefs about pricing and money. (That's why I never ask my mother what she thinks about my prices.) As money mindset mentor Denise Duffield-Thomas shares, "The reason why crowdsourcing really doesn't work is that most industries have collective insecurities and collective money blocks."[6]

On my podcast, Denise shared a delightful story about how she found a beautiful hand-carved stone box in a used book-store for only $14. Since the store priced it so low, she assumed it was secondhand. However, she learned that the owner's wife made the boxes and wanted the merchandise to be "affordable." But who decides what's affordable?

I joked with Denise that had she discovered the same box displayed on a crystal tray in a SoHo gallery, she'd gladly have paid $500 and considered that affordable. Denise went on to suggest that art need not be affordable, asking, "Why should art and beauty be so cheap that we burn ourselves out creating it for people? We live in this consumer society now, where we think that everyone should be able to afford everything they want, when they want it." In the end, because she paid so little for the box, Denise tossed it in her last Marie Kondo–inspired decluttering spree. She valued it less because she paid only $14 for it, but it was probably worth a lot more, especially since it was handmade.

Art pricing can feel arbitrary, which makes it difficult to price without letting your drama get in the way. I ask clients to try on a price to see how it feels. Think of your prices as a well-fitting pair of jeans. The prices should be high enough to make you feel a little uncomfortable, but not so high that you'll choke on your own vomit. In other words, you should be able to make the offer with a straight face.

Abundant Artist Lesson #3: Your art isn't a commodity.

Your buyers aren't looking for the lowest price—and they'll be excited by higher prices because they appreciate something exclusive that not everyone can afford. When you use low prices to distinguish your work, you're treating your art as a commodity, and a disposable one at that. But when you have a signature style and brand, your art will be incomparable.

commodity

a good or service that is easily replaced without regard to who produced it, such as sugar or salt

Dan Kennedy and Jason Marrs provide a great example of a good that's easily commoditized: women's underwear. If you want a pair of underwear just to cover your bum, the cheapest option is probably cotton Hanes packaged in a five-pack. These utility versions of full-coverage underwear come in a variety of patterns and colors, but mostly sell for function. While browsing the Walmart website, I sorted underwear by price, and found a Hanes ten-pack for $14.99 (about $1.50 per pair).

Now, since your art is probably not purely functional, like everyday underwear (and you don't have the scale to mass-produce items at a low cost the way Hanes does), you should never treat it like a commodity. I'm going to continue to thread more underwear examples throughout these lessons to help you understand how modern consumers now shop. As Cora Harrington writes on her popular blog *The Lingerie Addict*, lingerie is a way to "express your personal identity and sense of self," which makes it a great analogy for exploring why people buy art.[7] (Besides, fashion and lingerie are also art forms in and of themselves.)

Abundant Artist Lesson #4: Some buyers want what's most popular.

The default search engine setting on Walmart's website is "most popular," not "lowest price." Even price-conscious Walmart shoppers aren't necessarily looking to purchase the lowest-priced items. At the heart of making purchasing decisions, customers are worried about making a mistake—and for some, seeing what's popular eases that decision drama. That's why name brands—offering built-in social proof—are so appealing. Brands can also broadcast popularity by including testimonials on their websites or by using social media influencers through paid promotions. Research from Win BIG Media showed that what they call "influenced consumers" are 59 percent more likely to purchase items promoted by microcelebrities and prefer when brands are trendy.[8] Another way artpreneurs can convey demand is by sharing "sold" items as well as pictures of happy customers on their website and social media.

Abundant Artist Lesson #5: Make more money by offering bundles.

Hanes doesn't offer individual underwear priced at $1.49 per pair. They offer packages, or bundles, of multiple pairs. Just like Hanes, artists shouldn't sell things individually that could be sold as a package, set, or grouping. This applies whether you're selling note cards, lessons, coaching packages, prints, or even ceramics. Offer a set of six note cards, a six-month piano lesson package, or a ten-piece ceramic set. Offering sets isn't the same as using the "buy one get one" (BOGO) pricing strategy. BOGO is a starving-artist tactic that immediately cheapens your art. On the other hand, bundling is a classy way to encourage your customers to make a larger purchase.

When selling online art classes, I often group similar classes together and offer a discount when students purchase the bundle. This form of bundling helps you discount without cannibalizing your art or services. For my prints and original paintings, I extend a 10 percent "collector's discount" when clients collect more than one artwork. Again, this is a way to reward your best customers without devaluing your brand.

Many teachers commoditize their services and offer them in a way that lowers their earning potential. For example, a fully booked music teacher who charges $45 for a forty-five-minute private lesson would have to spend eight hours a day teaching, without vacation or time off beyond weekends, in order to generate an income of $90,000 a year. This also assumes that students are coming *to* our exhausted music teacher. If she must add travel time to the days, her workday is much longer than the time she's being paid for.

Teachers can make more money and work fewer hours when they make their work scalable, charging for group instruction. Using our music teacher example, an instructor who teaches just five hours a week but offers group classes can command the same income as the exhausted private teacher. In other words, you can work less and make more money. Remember, just like scattering seeds in a garden, easier can be better.

AVERAGE PRIVATE-TEACHING BUSINESS MODEL	GROUP-CLASS BUSINESS MODEL
40 lessons per week 1 student in a lesson 50 weeks $50 for a 45-minute lesson	5 group lessons per week 20 students in a group 50 weeks $25 per group lesson per student
Math: 40 × 50 × $50 = $100,000	Math: 5 × 20 × 50 × $25 = $125,000

You can see that the teacher who uses a group-class format and teaches just five hours a week will make $125,000, or 25 percent more than the exhausted private music teacher. You can also dramatically increase your teaching income by charging a premium for your services rather than average prices. Look at what a difference charging a premium for a private lesson makes. Simply by charging a premium, a teacher using higher pricing can also work less and make more money. Moreover, when teachers take their classes online, scaling becomes easier and more lucrative.

PREMIUM PRIVATE-TEACHING BUSINESS MODEL
20 lessons per week 1 student per lesson 50 weeks $125 for a 45-minute lesson
Math: 20 × 50 × $125 = $125,000

Abundant Artist Lesson #6: Repeat buyers spend more.

If price were customers' sole motivation, everyone would choose the cheapest underwear, right? Not necessarily. The only time I've ever reached for the $1.50 underwear is when I've had my period and didn't want to ruin the nicer ones. I consider those matronly pants throwaways.

What motivates a woman like me to spend four times the amount on underwear from a higher-priced brand like Victoria's Secret? I know the large cotton brief will cover my ample derrière and, unlike nylon lace, won't give me a rash. As much as I drooled over many of the lingerie brands I researched for this chapter, I'm sticking with my fuddy-duddy briefs because it gives me too much anxiety to experiment. In other words, I normally buy Victoria's Secret because I've bought from them before.

What does this mean for us artists? The customers most likely to buy from us are the ones who have already bought from us (as long as they had a good experience!). According to a 2020 study by investpro.com, the likelihood of selling to an existing customer is 60–70 percent, while the probability of selling to a new customer is 5–20 percent, and repeat buyers are also likely to spend 67 percent more.[11] This is why staying in front of your current customers with email marketing (and physical mail) is so important. We'll talk more about how to get started building an email list in chapter 8.

Abundant Artist Lesson #7: People pay more when they feel a connection to the maker.

Victoria's Secret underwear is four times the price of the Hanes brand, but it's still not considered high-end. Luxury retailer Neiman Marcus has a lingerie department and refers to underwear as "panties." They price their most popular panty, a black lace Natori, at thirty-two dollars, triple the Victoria's Secret price and twenty times the price you'd pay at Walmart. The description of the black Natori lace panty includes a bio of the brand's founder, Josie Natori. The two-sentence bio shares how Natori left the world of finance and built a global brand that marries the aesthetics of her Filipino heritage with a modern Western appeal. As someone who also left finance to build a business from my creativity, Natori's founder story immediately appealed to me and connected me with the brand. Perhaps that's why Natori is now one of the lingerie giants that covers a wide variety of price points, from those less expensive than Victoria's Secret all the way up to Neiman Marcus.

In order to create a connection with your prospects, you'll want to sprinkle your quirks, values, and weirdness throughout your website, online copy, and social media. After hitting your site's home page, the "About" page is the next place your prospect will likely go, so make sure to craft an engaging "About" page for your site. Also, consider sprinkling personal, relevant fun facts throughout your product listings, as in the Natori example. For example, on my "About" page I list seven fun facts, including "I'm vegan (most of the time) and lie about it the rest of the time."

Abundant Artist Lesson #8: Describe your item with how you want your buyer to feel.

Many lingerie brands use descriptive words that connote romance, seduction, and sex to describe their products. With its feminist founder story, the Natori brand went in a completely different direction, appealing to modern women who want to feel sophisticated—and their marketing copy is crafted accordingly. Successful brands use *feeling* words to describe their product. This company understands that their product could be a commodity, as something all women need to wear, but they're playing to our emotions, which is how they're able to command high prices. Of course, they're backing up the marketing with the highest-quality fabrics and materials—but when describing the products, they help us see that this luxury panty will make us feel different. People will pay more for a product that makes them feel good and gives them pleasure.

LINDA DOUCETTE HAD a thriving business selling her felted art and needlework at art festivals until COVID-19 shut down the festival circuit. She came to me looking for ways to sell her art online. However, once she resumed in-person selling after an eighteen-month hiatus, she found that her new strategies made selling easier even at higher prices. That is, using emotions to describe her art (rather than focusing on sharing her techniques) made all the difference. She said, "Yeah, I just came off a good show this weekend. Shockingly good. My price point was higher, and they were gravitating toward more expensive work. There was one thing that you said. 'Talk about the emotion of the piece, not the thing that it is.' I sold two pieces of winter scenes in the middle of August, talking about the serenity of the snow and the peaceful feeling and the hush of the night. And they're like, 'I'll take it!'"[12]

Abundant Artist Lesson #9: People pay more for status.

Neiman Marcus offers panties that are much more expensive than the popular Natoris. The highest-priced panty I found on their website was a Dolce & Gabbana leopard-print, stretch-silk Brazilian brief for $415, making this choice nearly three hundred times higher than Hanes and seventy times higher than Victoria's Secret. The founder's bio emphasizes the brand's association with celebrities, which increases the status of wearing Dolce & Gabbana. For this brand, the copywriters prioritized style and status rather than comfort.

Status via Queen Bee endorsements. You won't need celebrity endorsements if you've got the cool kids wanting what you've got. Here's how I managed this in the world of commissioned portraits. Each year, my kids' elementary school ran a fundraiser. This PTA-run event included a pricey country club dinner and a silent auction that ran during a cocktail hour. For the silent auction, I donated a portrait commission of one child in my starter size, and I placed my portfolio of portraits next to the bid sheet. Invariably, the cool girls competed to win the portrait. Usually, the winning family had more than one child, and I would make money on the additional figures painted. The real upside, though, was that the cool PTA mom was now a customer, and her child's portrait was added to my portfolio. All the wannabes in town coveted a portrait just like the Queen Bee of the PTA moms, which created a natural ecosystem for promoting my art.

Status via scarcity. One reason my classmate Suzie was so put out to see I had a "Gucci" watch was that she wanted to be the only one with that status symbol. Part of the appeal of high-priced items is the barrier to entry. In addition to higher prices, luxury brands create another barrier to entry by limiting the supply of their goods. For example, Chanel may design a range of handbags but will only place one of each style in a location so that customers fear missing out if they don't make an immediate purchase.

There's a women's clothing boutique just outside New York City that never puts anything on sale. The store owner shared with me that women come into the store asking for the newest arrivals. The store only stocks one item in each size, so each item is always the last one. When an item has trouble selling, they move it out of that store to its sister outlet a few towns away. Again, this strategy of never discounting and limiting supply trains their customers to make quicker purchasing decisions at full price.

Abundant Artist Lesson #10: Conscious consumers buy in alignment with their values.

Conscious consumers spend more money when they feel a brand is authentically in alignment with their values, such as equity and inclusion, sustainability, philanthropy, and ethical corporate practices. Research (again from Win BIG Media) demonstrated that brands that shared their values in their messaging attracted this group of consumers. Win BIG Media called this group "activist consumers"; however, the academic term is "consumer activist" or "conscious consumer."[13] This demographic is also 80 percent more likely to purchase from direct-to-consumer businesses, such as the small business owner on Etsy. And because of their propensity to support social justice causes, they're 151 percent more likely to shop from women- and minority-owned businesses. Conscious consumers cross multiple age demographics, from the college student all the way to the socially minded baby boomer.[14] Moreover, the data from Win BIG Media showed that 35 percent of this group has household incomes over $100,000, making this group high-value customers who would be highly likely to have the means to invest in discretionary purchases. This is another reason why leaning into your values, as discussed in the last chapter, is so important. Your values matter to your customers.

As Dolce & Gabbana has been called out on their cultural insensitivity,[15] conscious consumers who have the means for luxury lingerie might turn to an online marketplace such as Supernatural Lingerie, which showcases ethically sourced materials and features a body-inclusive variety of fashion models on their website. This lingerie website has underwear priced all the way up to $484, and checks a lot of boxes, as it is a women-run business that features independent designers using ethically sourced materials. Moreover, Win BIG Media's research also showed that the conscious consumer appreciates creativity in marketing, and this company's website has it in spades. They even allow buyers to filter lingerie by their respective zodiac signs.

Abundant Artist Lesson #11: Symbols and punctuation matter.

Have you ever noticed that fancy restaurants always round their prices? Sometimes they don't even use the currency symbol on the menu.[16] Researchers from the Cornell School of Hotel Administration found that people given a menu without dollar signs spent significantly more than those who received a menu with them.[17] This is because it reduced the transactional experience of the number. When I'm asked to quote prices online via email or messenger, I leave off the dollar symbol and the comma. For example, if a painting is $2,000, I quote the price to my customer as 2000 or 2000USD or sometimes even 2K.

Charm pricing versus prestige pricing. When I'm selling online art classes, I use what's known as "charm pricing." This is the practice of reducing the price to just under the threshold of the next price up. For example, I offer my Watercolor Portrait Academy class at $497—because art students, who are price-sensitive, perceive the price as a number in the four hundreds. I also avoid using numbers that end in 9, such as $499. Numbers that end in 9 signal value rather than quality. Ending the number with a 7 or a 5 feels friendlier. On the other hand, when I sell my paintings, I use a rounded number. For example, I'll price a painting at either $480 or $500 instead of $497. Using the rounded number is known as "prestige pricing."

A 2015 research study by Kuangjie Zhang and Monica Wadhwa proved that rounded numbers are processed by the feeling part of the brain, whereas non-rounded numbers (or those using charm pricing) are processed by the logical part of the brain.[18] Their research showed consumers were more inclined to buy a bottle of champagne when it was priced at $40.00 rather than $39.72 or $40.28. Which part of the brain do you want your customers using when buying your art? The feeling part of the brain.

When I sold my art on eBay, they advised sellers to price past the decimal point to increase sales. In other words, selling an item for $40.28 as in the example above. That's because eBay attracts bargain hunters. You'll notice that places like Walmart also price their offerings to the penny. They're telling their customers that pennies matter, and as a result they attract penny-pinching customers. When you're selling art, a luxury, you want to do the opposite and communicate quality. Jeffrey Shaw, portrait photographer to the rich and famous, says, "If you're going to price yourself down to nickels and dimes, then you can't complain about people nickel-and-diming. Because you're literally calling forward the nickel-and-dime-minded customer."[19]

Abundant Artist Lesson #12: Focus on the experience, not the transaction.

When you believe your customers are primarily motivated by price, you may end up killing sales because you risk turning the purchasing experience into a transactional one. Recently, one of my collectors, Eileen, had reached out by email because she was considering commissioning a painting for her penguin-obsessed high school daughter, Chloe. Previously, Eileen had decided against a penguin painting because rebellious Chloe had been giving her such a hard time that she didn't want to reward her daughter with a present. (Spoiler alert: Your customers are deciding whether they're worth the investment. In this case, my customer was considering whether she wanted to treat her daughter to original art—in other words, whether Chloe "deserved" it.)

To make Eileen feel good about investing in this art, I suggested we hop on the phone for a quick call to see what she had in mind. My taking the time to get on the phone signaled to Eileen that I was willing to make time for her, rather than try to close a sale through email. On our call, I began by asking where her daughter was going to college and what she planned to study. Since she had hesitated to collect art for Chloe in the past, I wanted to make sure Eileen stayed focused on Chloe's most recent accomplishments, not her past transgressions. (I was also careful not to turn the conversation to my own children, and I kept Eileen and her family the focus of the call.) Next, we discussed the kind of art she had in mind, including the size, and whether this art was planned for her dorm room or at home. Finally, with a clear vision of the art I'd make for Chloe, I was ready to present a price.

Often, when you reach this stage of the conversation, your buyer will ask for the price. This is their way of asking to buy. In this case, I offered the price and then asked how she wanted to pay. Taking the time to get on the phone with Eileen and make her feel heard made all the difference. Positioning the price as the last part of the conversation recentered the buying on the experience, rather than on the transaction.

Bring an attitude of connection to your sales conversations to keep them from becoming too transactional, and really listen to your customers. Listening is always more important than what you have to say. However, sometimes there are words (spoken and written) that repel customers because they feel "salesy." For example, the word "buy" has a negative connotation, whereas the word "collect" doesn't carry the same stigma. In chapter 9, you'll find a table that lists words to avoid, along with those you'll want to use instead, in addition to my exact sequence for selling.

Abundant Artist Lesson #13: Make purchasing easy.

There's a difference between minimizing the transactional experience and making it difficult for customers to pay you. When reviewing artists' websites, sometimes I have trouble figuring out how to buy their art. If a tech-savvy person has trouble navigating your website, imagine what the average buyer will experience. A confused mind never buys. Do yourself a favor and ask someone who isn't tech-savvy to test-drive your website without explaining to them what to do. If you feel the urge to give them verbal instructions or they get lost and can't figure out how to buy, those are sure signs that your website isn't easy to navigate, and you'll need to make it more user friendly.

Please make it easy for people to pay you. Your website should have clearly defined prices and a built-in shopping cart. Your prospects shouldn't have to contact you to learn the price of your goods and services, price of shipping, or options for size, shipping, and so on. Don't annoy by putting obstacles in the way of customers making an impulse purchase. Make the experience as simple and delightful as possible. In addition, you can minimize your customers' shopping risk to make them feel more comfortable buying from you by offering returns or refunds.

I recommend offering free domestic shipping, as this has become the norm online. Standard practice is to make sure your prices are high enough to cover shipping costs—and keep in mind that if the customer is able to do a local pickup, you won't have to ship your art, which means you'll earn a higher profit. If a customer chooses to come to your store or studio to buy, you don't need to offer a discount, because they'll be receiving better service when you take the time to help them make a decision. Your time always has value!

Abundant Artist Lesson #14: Give buyers space to make up their minds.

People considering an art investment aren't always mulling over whether the art or the maker is worth the high price tag; sometimes they're considering whether they themselves are worth investing in. Famed copywriter Ilon Specht understood this when she created the signature slogan for L'Oréal cosmetics: "Because you're worth it." She penned the phrase in 1971, out of frustration with a beauty industry focused on the male gaze.[20] She empowered cosmetics buyers to own their decisions. Over fifty years later, the brand makes no apologies about costing more than their competitors and retains the largest market share in cosmetics worldwide.[21]

When I see a customer on the fence, I don't rush in to convince them that my art (or my coaching package) is "worth it." If they already know that your program, product, or service is valuable but haven't yet convinced themselves of their *own* worth, your selling arguments will land flat. After you've presented the price, don't rush in to fill the uncomfortable silence with chatter. There's no need to convince anyone. Give your buyers the space to make up their own minds. People buy high-end art for the same reasons they buy gourmet food, luxury cars, beautiful clothes, and expensive homes. And, yes, expensive underwear. Art is beautiful, but more importantly, people buy art because of how it makes them feel, or because they like what collecting that art says about them. Art reminds people of their true values every day. Low price is *never* a reason to buy art. If someone didn't want your art for $100, they won't want it for $50 either. And sometimes people will want the art *more* if it's $1,000—because the higher price connotes prestige and value, which are motivators for luxury shoppers.

WHAT ARTPRENEURS NEED TO BELIEVE

- When you crowdsource your prices, you're essentially copying other people's limiting beliefs about pricing and money.
- Art connoisseurs are luxury buyers who assume higher prices denote value.
- When you use low prices as a distinguishing factor, you're treating your art as a commodity.
- At the heart of purchasing decisions, customers are worried about making a mistake.
- People will pay more when a product makes them feel good and gives them pleasure.
- Part of the appeal of high-priced items is the barrier to entry.
- When you believe your customers are primarily motivated by price, you risk turning the purchasing experience into a transactional one, which could kill the sale.

MARCHING ORDERS

- Make it easy for people to pay you by including
  e-commerce options on your website.
- After you've presented your price, don't rush in to fill the
  uncomfortable silence with sales chatter.
- Bundle your offers to create value for your buyers
  without cannibalizing your art or services.
- Sprinkle your quirks, values, and weirdness throughout
  your website, online copy, and social media in order to
  create a connection with your prospects.

"THE ROLE OF THE ARTIST IS EXACTLY THE SAME AS THE ROLE OF THE LOVER. IF I LOVE YOU, I HAVE TO MAKE YOU CONSCIOUS OF THE THINGS YOU DON'T SEE."

—JAMES BALDWIN

LOVE YOUR BUYER

C LARIBEL AND ETTA CONE, otherwise known as the Cone sisters, used their enormous family wealth and elite connections to amass a museum-worthy art collection.[1] Born during the American Civil War and Reconstruction era, as young women, the Baltimore sisters traveled abroad. On their trips to Paris, author and American expatriate Gertrude Stein introduced them to Parisian society, including her inner circle of artists like Matisse and Picasso. In those days, art collecting was rare among women—but these weren't ordinary women. Elder sister Claribel earned her medical degree decades before women were even allowed to vote. Younger sister Etta managed the family's household affairs. Their family's cotton mills supplied fabric for the military during World War I, and later served as the largest supplier of denim for Levi Strauss. Such was their enormous wealth —and their interest in art collecting—that they often bought an extra seat at the Paris Opera for their shopping bags of fine art and collectibles. On their second trip abroad after the war, they required an extra stateroom to house their considerable purchases, and when they returned home, they rented a second apartment to display their treasures. Artists dream of patrons like these taking an interest in their art.

Etta outlived her sister by twenty years and continued growing her collection. In the end, she bequeathed their entire art collection—more than three thousand objects, including more than seven hundred works by Matisse and more than one hundred by Picasso—to the Baltimore Museum of Art. So, why did the Matisses outnumber the Picassos? In the museum's 2021 exhibit "A Modern Influence: Henri Matisse, Etta Cone, and Baltimore," curators point to the forty-three-year friendship between Matisse and the Baltimore collector. Her friendship with the artist, and actively collecting his avant-garde work, including nude figures, "provided her with a sense of identity, purpose, and freedom from convention."[2] And through his frequent letters to Cone, Matisse nurtured this relationship consistently. He updated the heiress about his artist life with stories and pictures of his works in progress. He understood that, as the artist, it was his job to pursue the collector—not the other way around. He didn't wait in his studio, hoping to be courted by the sisters (Rapunzel-style marketing). He pursued them.

When you're looking to build your own audience of collectors and patrons, there's no better way than using the art of the letter or, in the modern artist's world, the humble email to build an audience of adoring fans. When you email people, you're not just marketing or selling; you're building a relationship.

COURTSHIP

Maybe you've heard the term "sales funnel" to describe the process of moving someone from prospect to paying customer. I prefer to think of taking my art collectors through a courtship rather than a sales funnel. Sounds more personal, don't you think? In this way, you take your ideal prospect on a journey that smoothly transitions them through each stage of your courtship—meeting you, flirting, going steady, falling madly in love, and, finally, committing to a purchase.

There are a number of avenues through which an artist/prospect relationship may begin. The prospect could be someone you know, a stranger at an in-person event, or someone browsing online. Just like meeting a potential true love on a dating app, don't expect a proposal on the first swipe. Even if it feels like love at first sight, it's unlikely someone will ask for your hand in marriage the first time you meet. Just as in dating, you'll need to court your prospect over time until they're ready to commit.

THE PICKUP ARTIST

Most selling venues, like outdoor fairs or even Etsy, aren't much different from singles bars or dating apps, with lots of potential matches for you. Some browsers—both online and in person—are there just to pass the time, while others are more serious about making a purchase. As in the singles scene, lots of people are not looking for commitment. When a pickup artist procures a phone number from a potential romantic partner, that's considered a score. And that's the same strategy that will work for you in selling. Let me explain.

Using the dating analogy, you'll quickly see that there are winning and losing strategies. Unfortunately, many artists tend to choose losing ones. Whether the meeting is online or in person, they imagine that their prospects will chase after them. But this isn't how buying psychology works. If a prospect likes your art—apart from the exception when she has fallen in love with something at first sight—you'll need to stay in touch and court your prospect for quite some time. Moreover, if you've sold your art on social media without a reliable way to stay in touch, then you're missing out on repeat buyers, as we discussed in abundant artist lesson #6 in chapter 7. Of course, in order to stay in touch with them via email marketing, you'll have to get them to give you their contact info (with their permission). This is the essence of prospecting.

STOP HANDING OUT BUSINESS CARDS

I cringe every time I hear an artist say that it was a great show because they gave out a lot of cards. When you're at an event and someone says, "Here's my business card," that's kind of like the desperate creep saying, "Here's my phone number." Yikes! Instead, ask for their number so you can control the next step. Just like dating. Sure, you could hope the prospect takes your number, which they didn't ask for, and calls you. (Or you can hope that this person may show up at the same place again, at the same time you do. Good luck with that. And even then, there's no guarantee.) But when you depend on your prospect to chase you, it's a gamble. Businesses that rely on channels (like Instagram) might make sales, but they won't necessarily get long-term customers because if they're not obtaining buyers' contact information, such as an email address, they have no way to get in touch with them outside of the platform.

If you've wishfully handed out lots of cards, don't feel bad. You're not alone; lots of artists do this—and I did this in the beginning too. Unfortunately, most often your prospect has tossed the card by the time they reach the next trash can. Some art-fair goers enjoy collecting cards, but most of them just ask for or accept your card as a polite way of gracefully getting away from you without making a purchase.

Maybe you're still not convinced that giving out your card is a losing strategy. If so, has anyone ever called you after taking your card? Or perhaps a better question to ask yourself: How many times have you saved a business card with the intention of purchasing an item, and gone back later to buy it? Did you even bother to go to the maker's website? Probably not. Chances are, you either tossed the card before you rounded the corner, or you still have it in the litter of your junk drawer, the bottom of a purse, or the floor of your car, but have long forgotten why you took it in the first place.

FLIP THE SCRIPT

I always use a prospect's request for my card as an opportunity to pivot and invite them to join my mailing list. Once I have their contact information, I have a modicum of control over the relationship. I can email them a thank-you note after the show, and then they'll get weekly emails from me in which I share new art. Often, I take it up a notch and send handwritten thank-you notes (with my art on them) to those people who share their physical mailing addresses. Of course, not everyone you meet will hand over all their contact info, and that's normal and okay. The ones who do are the people who love your art but perhaps aren't ready, the first day they meet you, to make a purchase. They may need more time to warm up to buying.

You'll also find that some people will hand over their email address but not their home address, and vice versa. There are even people who will give you neither of those addresses but will give you their phone number. This is a good thing; just be sure to call them to follow up. Sculptor Michael Alfano[3] takes it one step further and gets every potential client's cell phone number so he can follow up with a personal call. We so seldom use our phones for calling nowadays, but those who do, stand out.

If prospects don't give you their contact information, that's okay. It probably means they're just not that into you (or your products), and you'll find someone else. Not everyone is a perfect match for your art. Luckily, you only need a few prospects investing in your art *at premium prices* to make a sustainable living. If you learn nothing else from this book, remember that flipping the script from "contact information distributor" to "contact information gatherer" will make you more money as an artist in the long run.

EMAIL COLLECTION CARDS

Because people are very reluctant to add their email to a publicly displayed clipboard or list, to gather contact info in person I use email collection cards. Letting them fill out a card gives your prospect privacy and bestows more "giving" energy rather than "taking" energy. These cards are modeled after old-fashioned magazine subscription "blow-in" cards that fall out of magazines (and litter your floor). You can get them bulk printed in postcard size. The header would include some form of branding, but there's no need to create a fancy logo. On the top inch of my cards, I've used part of a painting and included my URL. If you're not a visual artist, fancy typography with your website address and your name will do the trick. Next, include a checkbox that says, "Yes, please send me updates!" followed by blank lines for prospects to enter their name, email and mailing addresses, and phone number.

Be sure to get these cards printed on matte card stock, since glossy postcards are impossible to write on. In addition, you can use the back of the postcard for taking notes. Always keep a handful of these on you for your successful elevator-pitch moments. You never know when you'll meet your next prospect!

JANE SMITH www.janesmithart.com

☑ Yes! Please send me updates about your art.

Name: _____

Email: _____

Mailing Address:

_____

_____

6 EASY WAYS TO GET SIGN-UPS
TO YOUR EMAIL LIST

You can't expect people to give you their personal information without a good reason. Yet I routinely see artists' websites telling me to "Subscribe to my newsletter!" or "Sign up for free updates!" Sorry, no one wants more email for no reason. That's why it helps to persuade people to sign up, with what's known, in marketing speak, as an "opt-in giveaway," "ethical bribe," or a "lead magnet." The idea is to give your prospects a free taste of what you offer in exchange for signing up for your email list. An example might be a free collector's guide, an e-book on how to create (if you're a teacher), or perhaps a guide on choosing an instrument. Most retailers offer discounts to new subscribers, but this tends to work only if the prospect already knows they want to purchase your item. The key is making sure you're giving people something that only people who like your art would want, and that will lead them to eventually make a purchase. Here are the six best ways for artists to get sign-ups.

Method #1: Ask them.

Remember those potential customers who asked for your card? That's your cue to ask them to join your list so you can send them an invitation to your next event. (That's as good a reason as any.) I encourage my clients to start asking anyone who takes an interest in their art to join their list. You can simply say, "I'd love to add you to my list so I can invite you to my next show."

These requests should take the form of a one-to-one interaction. Don't spam your friends by sending a bulk Facebook message or email. Keep in mind that when you ask someone to join your list, you're doing so from a place of sharing, not selling. And don't ask them to make a purchase the moment they hand over their contact information—like the creep who sends unsolicited pics on Instagram. Don't be that desperate.

Method #2: Create a free art catalog or e-book.

Create a simple PDF that includes prices, size details, and images of your products, or compile your best blog posts (including both text and images) into a single document. I've experimented with both printed and digital versions of my art catalog, and the digital version performs better and costs nothing. You can tell people who find you (both in person and online) that you can email them this freebie that introduces helpful information to new customers. You can update your freebie, and I do so often, which means you can send out another email to everyone already on your list with the newest version.

Method #3: Offer subscriber discounts.

Artist Megan Duncanson posts her subscriber sign-up link wherever she can.[4] It's the first post you see when you visit her anywhere online, strategically pinned to the top, offering exclusive subscriber discounts. Many brands offer coupons like that as incentives to join their list, but if your customer hasn't decided to buy yet, offering a coupon may not be as effective as the other strategies discussed here.

Method #4: Provide early access.

Landscape painter Emily Jeffords regularly sells out her collections within minutes of announcing their release via email. Collectors know that if they want to own an original, they need to be subscribed and open her emails. Between these launches, she also nurtures her collectors with emails and social media posts. By the time she releases a new collection, she has already posted photographs of the pieces, styled in her studio, and promoted the entire process for months.

Jeffords also generates anticipation by notifying her list about a new collection, the date and time the pieces will be live on her website, and some backstory on them. She then emails her list the day before the launch, and again in the final moments before the collection goes live. The final email is usually shorter and includes direct links to the artworks. "My email list is a wonderful way to connect with my collectors in a more thorough way than social media allows,"[5] Jeffords says. Like Matisse and Jeffords, you, too, can use the art of the letter to woo your customers. This strategy of notifying your list about a forthcoming collection launch is highly effective. You can tease your list that this collection is coming soon, the same way you see previews at the movies, and make a big deal about the release date, like it's opening night.

Method #5: Giveaways.

Abstract artist Amira Rahim builds her email list using Instagram giveaways of a free print.[6] The sign-up link to enter the giveaway and subscribe to her list is in her Instagram profile. Like Jeffords and Duncanson, she also offers early VIP access to newsletter subscribers. Using the VIP-access method, she launched and sold out a $4,000 collection within days of emailing her VIP subscribers. Some artists consider all their email subscribers VIPs, but you can also take this a step further and segment your list. I like creating a VIP list to segment who gets more emails than the rest of my list. These are the people who have (virtually) raised their hands and said they want to get notified first and more often. When you segment your list, you make your VIPs feel special, which will make them more likely to buy from you.

Method #6: Offer a free sample.

Although giveaways can work well, giving your prospect the opportunity to win isn't as effective as guaranteeing a gift or sample. Giving them something for free creates an open loop that triggers the human desire to reciprocate. That's why so many charities send you free address labels or note cards in the mail along with their solicitations to donate. The gift encourages charitable giving and buying.

Fine artists can send a free postcard (with their art on it, of course) as a gift for signing up. The key is to tell people the postcards are sent on a certain date in the future and only to active subscribers. Although sending a physical postcard is more of an investment than a digital freebie, I've found that collectors who are willing to give out their postal address are often the most enthusiastic and therefore more likely to purchase.

If you teach, you may want to let first-time students sample a free class or offer two classes for the price of one. Online teachers often offer a free class, in the form of a webinar or masterclass, to let new students sample their teaching style for free. Allowing prospects to get a free taste of what you offer is a great strategy. Think of it like the free samples bakeries leave out on the counter. Not everyone who takes a free sample will buy the whole cake, but you're more likely to get a sale this way.

KEEP IT KOSHER

Here's how you keep your email marketing kosher.[7] No matter the size of your list, you must use an email service provider that allows your prospects to unsubscribe at any time. This isn't the same thing as adding a sentence to the bottom of a mass email directing them to let you know if they no longer want to receive emails. If someone you're emailing doesn't want to be on your list and can't opt out in an automated way, then they're most likely going to mark your messages as spam. If enough folks do that, then even the people who want to receive your emails won't get them because Gmail (or another email service) will flag you as a spammer. Besides being uncool, sending bulk emails without permission or without a way for people to unsubscribe is illegal. The CAN-SPAM Act specifies that the email must contain an opt-out option for the recipient such as a clear and conspicuous "Unsubscribe" button or a "Change Preferences" link.

EMAIL MARKETING SOFTWARE

The specific software you use isn't as important as how frequently you use it. (Currently, the most popular email service providers are Mailchimp and ConvertKit.) Every email marketing program out there has pros and cons. For example, Mailchimp is more visually appealing whereas ConvertKit makes creating more complicated marketing campaigns easier. But Mailchimp isn't the most intuitive to use, and many artists get frustrated by it. I use Mailchimp, but if I were starting all over again, I'd probably pick something else. However, after so many years of building automations with this software, it's too much work for me to pack up all my toys and move to a different sandbox. Don't be seduced by the idea that if only you had such-and-such software, all your problems would disappear. Pick one and stick with it.

START SIMPLE

When you're just starting out, there's no need to create fancy automations. An automation is a series of emails that will be sent out based on an event such as someone joining your email list. For example, you can create a welcome sequence that has a series of three emails that go out automatically to new subscribers. This series will introduce you to your new subscriber, tell them what you're about, and start building a relationship. You'll be manually adding emails of everyone you meet in person. Likewise, you can manually enter email addresses for people with whom you interact online. The best way to do this is to talk about your freebie in a post and encourage those who are interested in it to "DM" you. Once you're talking to a prospect in your DMs, treat that interaction the same way you do when you're in person. Get their email address and do them the favor of taking the time to add it to your list. Even those who have the technical savvy to build complex automations agree. For example, Ryan Deiss, CEO of Digital Marketer, "believes the future of digital marketing belongs to companies that are willing to invest in real-time, one-to-one interactions."[8]

GET FANCY LATER

In order to gather email addresses in a more automated way, you'll need to create a web page that explains what you're going to give prospects in exchange for that email address. This is also known as a "landing page" and should feature a form where your prospect can enter their name and email. This form links to your email service provider and sends your prospect what you promised them. Because there are so many different website builders and email service providers to choose from, getting these two parts to connect may be challenging. You can always find someone to do it for you on a site like Upwork.com or Fiverr.com. However, when you choose popular service providers such as Mailchimp for your emails or Squarespace for your website, there are readily available tutorials online for you to do it yourself.

WHY DO I NEED EMAIL IF I HAVE SOCIAL MEDIA?

The only thing I find more cringeworthy than the artist who gives out lots of business cards is the artist who expects customers to find them on their social media accounts. If anything, relying on social media is the *least* dependable method of selling. Even if you develop a large following, you can't depend on these sites to show your content to your would-be sweethearts. Unfortunately, social media has been designed to get users to scroll and stay engaged until they're served an ad. These platforms are also designed to get you (the content provider) to purchase ads for your own products. You can increase the chances of getting people's attention by sharing compelling content on a regular basis, but there's no guarantee that your prospects are even going to see your posts. According to a 2022 report from Rival IQ, the average engagement rate across all industries is a measly 0.68 percent with influencers faring slightly better with an engagement rate of 1.18 percent.[9]

In addition, Meta's apps have been losing relevance as social media platforms while TikTok has gained in popularity. According to a Cloudflare report from the end of 2021, TikTok's traffic had surpassed Google's.[10] The point here isn't to go running to a new social media platform, but any business that relies on "rented land" is at risk of depending on strategies that will stop working in the future. Remember, TikTok was nearly shut down in the United States by executive order in 2020. When Instagram changed their algorithm in 2022 to prioritize videos over photos in the feed, many small businesses were hurt. Sana Javeri Kadri, who sells spices, regretted her reliance on Instagram; she shared in a *New York Times* interview, "I completely credit them for our growth—and then the algorithm changed, and our sales dropped horrifyingly." She went on to say, "It's been terrifying because I was really good at taking beautiful photos and writing long emotional captions and suddenly, for the past six months I've been mourning the loss of value of that skill."[11]

A better strategy is to get your followers to sign up for your mailing list. Although I have thousands of followers on Instagram and Facebook, my organic posts usually reach only a few hundred of my followers, a teensy fraction. Unless you pay for advertising, these platforms are increasingly difficult to use for keeping the attention of new prospects.

Before you whine that all this isn't fair, consider your own behavior on social media. If you're on these platforms, you likely follow hundreds of friends and brands. Can you imagine how impossible it would be to see every single one of their posts, even if you wanted to? You would have to spend hours on each platform to see the posts of everyone you're following. No matter how much time you spend on social media, there's no way to keep up with it all, and your followers aren't spending that much time keeping up with you.

Your followers are also following hundreds or even thousands of their favorite brands, artists, and celebrities, not to mention their friends and family. That's why social media platforms have an algorithm to prioritize which posts users see first. They do that by figuring out how often a user has engaged with a person or a brand's content. However, because these platforms show your posts to so few people, unless you pay for additional advertising, it's usually not worth your effort to make those posts more engaging. That's why this book teaches you how to market without relying on social media. Building an engaging email list of people who want to hear from you is much more effective.

MARKETING-NERD SPEAK

An algorithm is basically a behind-the-scenes math formula, but you don't need to know math or formulas to understand this. When I log on to Instagram, I usually see pictures of my nephew first. That's what I'd like to see, so thank you, Instagram, for knowing that. I also see posts from my daughter, who prefers posting cat videos, and my son's adventures in Israel. This creates a good experience for me and has me coming back day after day. I look forward to new cute pics of my redheaded nephew, his lips stained purple with Popsicle juice dripping down his chin.

If I saw an Anthropologie model sucking in her cheeks every time I logged on to Instagram, I don't think I would use the platform as much. Sure, I like a good boho dress, but do I want to see that before my cute baby nephew or my children? Absolutely not. Social media shows you posts by your friends, followed by popular posts, based on the engagement those posts have already gotten, and posts by accounts you've recently liked. If an Anthropologie post goes viral, Instagram might want to show that to me over a Kate Spade post, but they're not going to show me an Anthropologie organic post before they show me posts from my family. Social media platforms (including YouTube) work on these algorithms, and if you continuously like posts from an apparel brand such as Anthropologie, they'll serve you additional content and ads from other brands that post similar content.

CONNECTION COUNTS

Currently, social media algorithms also consider whether you have sent direct messages to brands or people, because the algorithm knows you've got more of a connection with them. That's why smart marketers will ask you to DM them. Not only will doing so form a stronger connection with their brand, but also, you'll be more likely to see their future posts.

Whether a direct message trumps the algorithm or not, the important thing to remember is that a DM is a one-to-one connection that goes a long way toward nurturing the client or collector you're courting. The most valuable thing I do on Instagram is to welcome new followers and ask them how they found me. After a few back-and-forth messages, I ask them if they have one of my latest freebies and then share the link to get it.

SOCIAL MEDIA IS A DEMANDING MISTRESS

Remember, though social media gets the attention of new people, the scroll isn't where authentic, deeper connections develop. Sure, art is sold on Instagram all the time, but those lucky sales are more like one-night stands than long-term relationships. In Instagram's early years, artists who relied heavily on the platform saw their income evaporate when Instagram demanded that they become full-time "Instagram artists." Meaning that in order to be "seen" by the algorithms, they had to create more and more content. In a 2020 blog post, artist Rachel Reichenbach shared details of a conversation she had with an Instagram employee. He advised Rachel to create four to seven reels per week, post on stories twice a day, and upload three long-form videos per week and three posts per week. The amount of content expected from the platform translated into artists making their dedication to Instagram a full-time job.[12] As social media expert Italina Kirknis says, "Instagram is a demanding mistress."[13] Social media platforms reward artists who spend increasingly greater amounts of time providing content for their platforms, and artists just can't keep up with creating digital content. The more time they spend creating content for social media, the less time they have to create their art. But there *is* a better way, which we'll get to shortly.

THE BLONDE ON THE NEXT BARSTOOL

Social media's role is to get attention for your art and your brand. Once you've embraced all that's weird and wonderful about you and your art, you'll have no trouble grabbing attention. But you don't need to be on every platform: pick the one or two that you truly enjoy. Most of an artist's time shouldn't be spent on these platforms anyway, and they should *never* be relied on for sales. Just as in dating, there will be lots of people to meet, but you're also competing with the blonde on the barstool next to you.

With that in mind, when you do post, show up as your most authentic self. Imagine you're meeting someone at a party. Don't make the conversation all about you. Ask them questions and get them to interact with you. Most important, since they may take an interest in you and want your "number," in advance, make sure your bio on these platforms includes a link to sign up for your email list.

Merely sharing a link to the home page of your website inside your bio is insufficient; you need to lead your prospects to the *exact* page on your site where they'll learn what they get in exchange for signing up for your email list—because if they get lost or confused on your site, they'll leave without doing anything, and they may never find you again. Consider engaging with new followers via direct messaging and asking them to join your email list. When I wrote this chapter, I had more than 23,000 followers on Instagram, and I still use direct messaging to engage with new ones. I no longer enter their email addresses by hand, but when you're starting out and your following is smaller, it's worth doing.

Don't send people to your website to buy something before you've gotten their email address. Your website is where you close the deal. Since they aren't likely to make a purchase the first time they meet you, you want to get their email address to stay in touch. Otherwise, you may never meet again.

WHY EMAIL IS STILL KING

Out of all the electronic marketing methods, email is the most reliable way for your messages to get through. The average open rate for emails hovers around 18 percent. That means 18 percent of your email list will see your message. Compare that to the less than 1 percent of your followers who see your posts on social media.

Your subscribers get to decide whether they'll open your email. When you share a post on social media, it's the social media app that decides whether to show your post to your followers. This is why when it comes to nurturing relationships, email remains king of the internet. In addition, I would argue that most people probably check their email inbox several times a day but take intermittent breaks from social media. (I know I do.) And even if they log on frequently, again, they're only seeing what the algorithm feeds them when they refresh. I've deleted social media apps from my phone to improve my productivity, but I would never delete the email apps from my phone. Email feels manageable because when I open an email, there's an end to it, whereas social media is an endless scroll of infinite distractions. When your subscribers read your email, they, too, are inside a container that has fewer distractions than social media, and it allows them to decide to take action before bouncing to the next thing.

In addition, email is even replacing blogging as the message platform of choice. In years past, bloggers would send a teaser email to their list to tell them to click over to a blog post. Now, many bloggers skip that step. With a platform such as Substack, their email subscribers *pay* to receive their emails (and Substack takes a 10 percent cut).[14] Some bloggers still post on their website, but instead of using clickbait to their list, they treat the email as the blog post. I encourage you to treat your emails in the same way. Tell the whole story inside your email (which you'll provide for free, unless your art is writing). Instead of teasing your readers to get them to go to a blog post, take your readers to where you sell your art on your website. You can still publish blogs separately on your website but treat the email as the main content platform.

LOVE LETTERS

To turn a onetime buyer or a looky-loo into a loyal patron, you need to stay in touch. For this purpose, there's only one avenue better than email—and that's the mailbox outside the front door. There's no spam filter in a snail mailbox and getting a personalized message into the hands of a potential buyer for the cost of a postage stamp is a small price to pay.

If there's an in-person component to your business, consider sending a handwritten note after meeting each new prospect. Sending invitations to your in-person events through physical mail is also effective. Since printing (and postage) is an investment, I'm more discriminating about who gets these invitations, and more aggressive about sending physical mail to people who have collected or commissioned art in the past. I also send physical cards to prospects who have recently signed up for my updates. Although I print these as affordable postcards, I spend the extra money to put them in an envelope to make sure they get opened rather than lost in the shuffle of junk mail. I've also used physical mail to engage my online clients and art students, sent "save the date" postcards to fill up webinars, and even turned sales pages for my online classes into printed booklets mailed to my hottest prospects.

The sales I made via direct physical mail more than paid for the cost of postage and printing, and my clients love the high-end touch. We get so little physical mail these days that artists who use the snail mail approach will stand out.

I make sure I tag all my collectors in my database as having attended an art show so I can send them an email invite to the same event every year. Think of your email service provider as a customer database whose fields (sometimes called tags) you can use to store information about your prospects and customers. Moreover, most email service providers know where their users live based on the subscriber's IP address. The geographical information is known as a geotag, and it allows you to send emails to people living in specified regions. If you have an in-person event in, let's say, Greenwich, you can invite only people who live within driving distance. To make this email even more personal, I may use a subject line like "See you in Greenwich?" This is guaranteed to get their attention because it feels so personal. Using a combination of geotagging and my own tagging system allows me to remind local collectors about events at venues near them. My email service charges me a monthly fee based on the number of subscribers I have on my list, but it doesn't charge me more to send additional emails. So, I send lots of email reminders.

+ + + MINDSET CHECK-IN + + +

What's coming up for you? Write down all your fears and doubts about sending emails. Are you worried about "bothering" people?

Label your thought distortions:

Mind reading = MR | Fortune-telling = FT
All-or-nothing thinking = AON

Notice which thoughts aren't serving you.

DRAG YOUR ASS OUT OF THE HOUSE

As an introvert, I know how comfortable it is to stay in your studio and create. However, when you have an upcoming event, such as an art show, a book launch, or a performance, in the days leading up to your event, force yourself to get out and into the "real world." Even if I've invited hundreds of people to an event, it's often the ones I've invited at the last minute in person—such as in a yoga class, or a happenchance meeting—who show up (and are most excited to purchase). That's why I keep a bunch of printed invitations in my purse for whenever an impromptu invitation opportunity presents itself. Drag your ass out of the house. Your audience is out there waiting to meet you. When you get out of the house and do your normal stuff, you'll naturally network and meet people who become prospects and eventually your customers.

HAPPILY EVER AFTER

In case you have doubts about whether sending snail mail really makes a difference, rest assured that my art collectors say it does. Many prospects show up to my shows clutching the post-card to their chest and thanking me for thinking of them—and they almost always purchase something.

In between shows, throughout the year I stay in touch with all my collectors via regular email updates, which I send at least once a month, or as frequently as every week. The emails include the same sorts of content that artists post regularly on social media. They include personal anecdotes, work-in-progress pictures, and stories about art collectors. These emails often lead to sales. During holidays, or when I'm running a promotion for an event like Black Friday or an online class launch, I may even email daily.

You might be concerned that all this email is bothering people. During the early days of the pandemic, and at the height of the social justice protests in 2020, a lot of sellers were afraid to continue sharing their work and emailing their list. I urged my clients not to stay quiet, as people were craving connection more than ever. At that time, I interviewed email list-building expert Amy Porterfield and asked her what she thought. She shared, "Right now, during a crisis, during a time when we are all asked to social distance and stay far away from each other, I think more than anything, we need community, we need engagement. As artists, it's so important that you put yourself out there and show up and say, 'Hey, I'm still here.'"[15]

If you want to build an audience of adoring fans, remember that when you email people, it can't just be about marketing or selling to them. It's about building that relationship, and, in that way, emailing collectors isn't bothering or bugging them. You don't need to take my word for it; listen to one of my clients, Canadian artist Patrick Guindon, who said, "I've received responses from people saying, 'I love that you're showing up for us more.' And so I'm like, 'Oh man, I thought I was bugging you. And I'm not bugging you, right?'" He also added, "The more raw and vulnerable I am, the more universal it seems to be. The more people respond, the more people hit 'Reply,' and it's blowing my mind. I'm finding that when I pick something that I care very deeply and passionately about, that's what people respond to."

When limiting beliefs prevent you from sharing your work through email or mail, do the work of examining those thoughts. Are they true? Are you mind reading or fortune-telling? If you assume people don't want to hear from you, then you're mind reading. Amy Porterfield understood and addressed this reluctance. "You could say, 'Well, this is my time to get quiet. Who's going to buy art right now?' Or you could say, 'This is when they need me most. I'm going to show up as my best self.' Obviously, you've got two choices; one is going to empower you and your audience so much more. It's important to have a voice right now. People need you."[16] You need to treat your prospects the same way you court a romantic partner or treat a friend, and you wouldn't ghost someone for three months because times were difficult and then expect them to still be interested.

CALL ME MAYBE

Are you ready to propose yet? To close a high-end sale, sometimes you may have to use your phone as a phone. This can be tricky, since many people no longer answer their phones; however, a conversation—or even a voice mail—can go a long way. I've even used an online tool to send personalized video messages. Depending on how well you're connected with your collector, you can also send a Facebook or Instagram video or voice message. These methods will work better if your prospects have already been "going steady" with you by reading your emails or engaging with your online content.

Why do phone calls work so well toward accelerating the nurturing process? Consider the many ways a call can help. For example, I mentioned that the people most likely to show up to my in-person events are those to whom I've given impromptu last-minute invitations in person. But what about the people who you haven't run into for a while, who you'd like to motivate to get to your local event? Pick up the phone and use it like a phone! This absolutely works. Or, at the very least, send them a text message.

Call your friends. Text your friends. Invite them to come even if you don't expect them to buy anything. If you're worried about pestering them, think of it as inviting your friends to hang out with you. Sometimes they'll make a purchase, but even if they don't, your booth now has people in it, which creates magnetic energy. When other customers come by, they're more likely to make a purchase because of that beautiful energy.

Will this work for you? It absolutely can. Try it! I've even sold high-end coaching packages for thousands of dollars by using personalized messages. It's important to make sure prospects feel that the message is intended just for them. Toward that end, I generally start the message with their name. And if the message is a video, it's great to use the picture-in-picture feature, which records your face and the image of the art (or service) you're selling at the same time. When I'm looking to connect with a client for a coaching program, I often record my video while screen-sharing their website so I can demonstrate that I've visited their site. There are so many ways to market creatively when you're nurturing prospects!

The moral of this story is to make sure you call people. I always try to make sure that people who have bought my work in the past know that my art event is taking place. But, believe it or not, many artists skip this critical step. The following true story illustrates just how important this is.

Karen spends thousands of dollars at my town's art show each year. Even when the event is publicized (somewhat), there's no guarantee that everyone sees the promotions or knows about the show. I usually send my own postcards to collectors to invite them to shows. Since Karen had bought from me in the past, I've called her to let her know when shows are coming up. Apparently, she appreciates my personal invitation so much that she often spends several hours looking through all my artwork and choosing the pieces she likes best. Of course, she collects other people's art as well because she likes to collect. But if I hadn't called her, none of us would have made any of those sales. Again, make sure you call people! They won't always pick up the phone, but you can still leave a message. And if it's a good friend, just send a text that says, "Hey, I would love it if you stopped by and just kept me company, and I can show you my new art."

These techniques work. Whether it's an art show, a book launch party, a concert, a poetry reading, or some other event, your friends and past patrons want to be included. Invite them from a place of love and connection.

LENGTH OF THE COURTSHIP

Without additional nudges from me beyond weekly emails, it can take up to six months to nurture an email subscriber until they finally collect art. Using more direct techniques accelerates the process. When a prospect has been following you for a while, they may want to invest in your art at your next event. This is because you've been nurturing the relationship for enough time, and they're primed to take the next logical step.

GOING STEADY

It's common for buyers who return to the same venue each year to step up their purchases. This happened when I met Anne and David at their children's music school, where I sold my art every year at the annual holiday boutique. The first year we met, they bought a little hand-painted box. It was a small thing, a thirty-dollar item. I don't even sell those anymore. After they bought it, their names went into my database for my postcards and weekly emails. When Anne and David returned to the holiday boutique the following year, they remembered me because of the continued connection, and they collected a print. Again, I stayed in touch and sent them personalized reminders just before the annual holiday show, letting them know I would be there.

With each email or postcard they received, they enjoyed a sneak peek or a coming attraction of what I planned to bring to the show. Each communication ramped up their interest. The third year they visited my booth, they invested in an original painting. After appreciating the kind of enjoyment they got from that first print, they valued the habit of art collecting and have made collecting my art at the annual show a family tradition.

In marketing-nerd terms, this is known as the "ascension model." Online marketers know that if they can get buyers to make a small purchase, often they'll be able to sell more expensive items to the buyers over time. But this only works if you stay in touch with your prospects and nurture the relationships.

WHAT ARTPRENEURS NEED TO BELIEVE

- Silence does not mean "no." It could mean "not now." And "not now" could eventually turn into "yes."
- Learn to think of your chosen social media platform as an online dating app, and only the first step in a meaningful relationship.
- In our overconnected, noisy world, people need personal connections now more than ever.

MARCHING ORDERS

- Focus more on one-on-one connections and less on building massive followings.
- Collect all the contact information you possibly can from anyone you meet (online or in person) who likes your art.

- Create tags in your email system so you can send relevant reminders to people most likely to be interested in your event—and send thank-you notes to those who attended.
- For each of your events, make a "hot list" of people you want to call or text an invitation. This list should include hot prospects, repeat customers, and good friends.
- Make a "warm list" of your "not nows" to follow up with later.
- Between events, identify people who have expressed interest in your art and reach out to them directly.

"I'VE LEARNED THAT PEOPLE WILL FORGET WHAT YOU SAID, PEOPLE WILL FORGET WHAT YOU DID, BUT PEOPLE WILL NEVER FORGET HOW YOU MADE THEM FEEL."

—MAYA ANGELOU

SELL HAPPY ENDINGS

IN 1997, MASTERCARD LAUNCHED A thirty-second commercial featuring a father taking his son to his first baseball game. A male narrator rattled off all the purchases they made that day and their values: tickets, twenty-eight dollars; hot dogs, popcorn, and soda, eighteen dollars; and even an autographed baseball, forty-five dollars. In the second half of the commercial, the narrator shared the value of the conversation between father and son: "priceless."

Since that commercial aired and captured our imaginations, Mastercard has repeated this "priceless" formula using different characters and scenarios. In the final fifteen seconds of every commercial, the company sells us on emotions. No mention of the credit card's terms or its interest rates. The focus is on the feeling that a purchase can create. As our minds associate the happy ending of a father and son bonding (plus similar happy endings in all the commercials) with the Mastercard brand, the promotion forges a connection between potential customers and the credit card. If a company can create an emotional connection to their small piece of plastic, then certainly we artists can use emotion to sell our art. Like those last few seconds of every Mastercard commercial, creating an emotional connection to your art is what leads to sales. In order to improve your selling, think about how to promote the emotions your art may generate for customers.

PAIN OR PLEASURE

There are two reasons—and only two reasons—why people will buy anything. Either the product or service solves a problem, or it gives them pleasure. For example, aspirin cures a headache (removes pain), while chocolate and wine provide pleasure. With the arts, from music to painting and poetry, the general rule is that consumption of the arts brings pleasure. That doesn't mean the subject matter has to be rainbows and daisies; after all, people take pleasure in horror films, dark humor, goth art, and emo music. But ultimately your art is a product that makes people feel good, and you want to emphasize that happy ending.

The pleasure-versus-pain principle can be expanded into four major levers that drive all buying decisions. The levers are not only pain relief and pleasure but also investment and esteem.

BUYING LEVER	PURPOSE
PAIN RELIEF	Buyers have a pain they want removed, or a problem fixed. The art makes the home warm and inviting rather than cold and impersonal.
PLEASURE	Just as wine, chocolate, and flowers make people feel good, buyers want a work of art because it makes them feel good.
INVESTMENT	Some forms of art are investments for monetary gain. As a self-representing artist, it's best to remind customers how the art is an investment in themselves.

| ESTEEM | Buyers want the art because they want a piece of the maker, or the maker's celebrity—as well as what purchasing the brand says about them. |

Most marketing experts recommend that marketers focus on the pain: all those fears and anxieties that keep people up at night and give them night sweats. But I never understood how that advice would help me sell more art—or even motivate people to enroll in an art class. I couldn't imagine anyone lying in bed at night fretting about securing art for their hallway, or how to paint tulips. Even when I paid big bucks to ask the "gurus" for advice, they told me my buyer's pain point (the pain my art would help them solve) was a blank wall. That was terrible advice since a cheap mirror easily solves that problem.

If you're focused only on how your art solves a problem (using language like "Fill your wall!"), you're focused on the lowest value your art can provide. Sometimes focusing on a problem just doesn't make sense. Flowers, cookies, and art are sold by reminding buyers of the pleasure they'll receive. For example, you may have the problem of boredom, but no movie promoter would say, "Watch the new *Harry Potter* movie! It alleviates boredom!" That would be ridiculous. Instead, creators and promoters focus on how books, movies, music, dance, and art elicit pleasurable feelings. So the most effective way to inspire people to purchase your art (and pay big bucks for it) is to focus on their wet dreams, not their night sweats. For example, it's for pleasure that collectors eagerly pony up thousands of dollars for a felted chicken stool that might impress their friends when they entertain, or simply prompt them to crack a smile at the end of a long day when they prop up their tired feet. Sure, you can prop your feet on a pile of books—but a whimsical footstool in the shape of a chicken: priceless.

Remember that although it's okay to talk about how your art fulfills a need, toilet paper also fills a need. Again, Mastercard doesn't discuss in their commercials how carrying around the credit card allows the dad to not have to hit the ATM or carry a wad of cash. All those needs that the credit card meets aren't mentioned at all during the commercial. Put most of your attention on how your product gives buyers pleasure. For example, instead of emphasizing the pain of the blank wall, fine artists can emphasize the pleasure of showing off a beautiful home in time for the holidays.

Art can solve a problem and give pleasure at the same time. Prominent classical trumpeter for the LA Philharmonic Thomas Hooten offers private lessons and workshops to supplement his performance income. He rejects commoditizing his musical instruction and charges $250 for a thirty-minute Zoom lesson. Hooten recognizes that his reputation allows him to command these premium prices. His website copy emphasizes that budding musicians will learn to overcome their audition anxiety (the pain point). However, to the amateur high school trumpeter who dreams of one day performing with a major orchestra, the cachet of studying with a world-renowned musician is much more of a core selling point and is how Hooten commands high prices. The pleasure of studying with a superstar in this niche provides a thrill, and the name recognition adds esteem, an additional buying lever. If a buyer has a positive association with a celebrity and a brand, the art sells more easily.

Hooten's cachet is a significant buying lever for aspiring trumpeters aware of his reputation. If you're not familiar with the world of classical trumpet players, you may never have heard of Hooten, but being a household name isn't required to become a well-known figure. You can develop status for yourself by getting local press opportunities and attract raving fans by dialing in your quirks. That's why your signature style and brand matters so much.

The investment angle drives the prices of high-end art at auction because of the possibility that the art can later be resold at a higher value. Since your art is unlikely to be sold this way, consider how your buyer is investing in a better version of their current or future selves. Etta Cone didn't collect Matisse's art for its resale value. In fact, she donated her entire collection to the Baltimore Museum. However, with each Matisse purchase, she reaffirmed a vision of herself as a modern woman with the taste and means to build a world-class art collection.

MASLOW'S HIERARCHY OF NEEDS

To better understand buyer psychology, it helps to understand psychologist Abraham Maslow's hierarchy of needs.[1] His theory of human motivation consists of a five-tier model of human needs, often depicted within a pyramid—with the most basic needs at the bottom, and more complex needs above. Working up from the pyramid's bottom, the needs are physiological, safety, love and belonging, esteem, and self-actualization. For artists, making sure your creations fulfill a need from the latter three, more complex tiers of the pyramid will yield the most success. To do this, you'll need to focus on not just what you're selling but how you talk about what you sell, making sure you tap into these psychological triggers.

Physiological Needs

Physiological needs are biological requirements for human survival, such as food, drink, shelter, clothing, warmth, sex, and sleep. Products that satisfy a physiological need, such as clothing or bedding, can meet this need easily. But connecting to points higher on the pyramid will create greater demand for a product and justify higher prices, such as luxury lingerie or linen brands. If you're selling fine art, fine furniture, or handcrafted home goods, you can emphasize that your art *enhances* the home. This will raise your product from simply meeting a physiological need to meeting the higher needs we'll discuss below.

Safety

After a person's basic physiological needs are met, they next crave safety and security. Few works of art will satisfy this need, but it's still helpful to be aware of this motivator. For example, to sell more art, sprinkle the word "safe" throughout your marketing copy, as in: "Art will be safely shipped." Though you're not referring to the customer's personal safety, the word "safe" is a known positive psychological trigger, which is why you'll notice commercials often use the words "safe and effective." Another word marketers use to promote a sense of safety and well-being is "protected," as in: "You're protected by a money-back guarantee."

You'll find a complete list of power words at the end of this chapter. Sprinkle these words throughout your copy as a subtle signal to help your buyers feel safe and minimize perceived risks, especially if they're making a big purchase.

Love

After physiological and safety needs have been fulfilled, the third level of human needs involves feelings of love and belonging. This need for interpersonal relationships often motivates buying behavior. When collecting a nonessential item, such as art or one-of-a-kind handcrafted goods, people often prefer to collect from friends and family because of a strong personal connection. They love the art because they love the person who made it, and the art also represents their connection with the artist.

I've invested in more hand-felted scarves than I could possibly wear, simply because my friend Janet Sikirica[2] made them. Yes, they're gorgeous and I love the way they look, but it's the relationship that served as a catalyst to the sale. My friends collect art from me for the same reason. This is why nurturing your prospects as you would a friend is critical for moving them closer to a sale. For the 2021 Matisse show, curators from the Baltimore Museum presented a mountain of historical evidence that Matisse nurtured a forty-three-year friendship with his best art collector, Etta Cone. Matisse made beautiful art, but so did Picasso. Etta Cone collected far more art by Matisse—because *the relationship matters.*

Buyers might also be motivated to purchase from someone who isn't their "real life" friend, but whom they feel they know because of the artist's celebrity. Fans of my podcast, *The Inspiration Place*, may feel as though they know me because I'm with them when they're walking their dogs, driving to work, or going to the gym. The podcast allows me to express my philosophies and connect with other artists who feel aligned with my values. Podcasts aren't the only way, or necessarily the best way, to create a relationship with customers for your art or creative service. You can also draw in your dreamboat customers with blog content or a YouTube channel. You can nurture your relationships with followers through your weekly emails, sharing stories and photos of your works in progress. If you don't work in a visual medium, pictures of you at work can add that visual element to your regular updates. Treat these interactions as you would a conversation with a close friend, sharing honestly and authentically.

Belonging

On the same hierarchy plane as love is the feeling of belonging. For art collectors and other luxury buyers, feelings of belonging might be motivated by the kinds of purchases their friends make. In college, it might have been a Monet reproduction taped to your dorm room wall, and in some economic circles, a cute, mass-produced canvas print sourced from HomeGoods will do the trick. However, in elite circles of society, nothing but original art will do.

When American sisters Etta and Claribel Cone bought that extra seat at the Paris Opera to hold their shopping spree bounty, they demonstrated to society what they were up to. Certainly, they could have paid a courier to discreetly send their packages back to the hotel. Instead, by creating a scene with the extra seat, they invited gossip and notoriety. These same shenanigans go on today as influencers publicly display their "outfits of the day" on Instagram. People enjoy showing off their purchases. You can use this psychology to your advantage by tagging your customers on social media and giving them shout-outs.

My favorite part of watching home tours is watching celebrities proudly show off their art collections and explain why they collected their pieces. For example, Misty Copeland collects art from African American artists such as Deborah Roberts, Lorna Simpson, and Asuka Anastacia Ogawa. For Ms. Copeland, sharing a connection to these artists' cultural heritage made a difference to her collecting.[3] Likewise, artists Shepard Fairey and Jon McNaughton have fostered a sense of belonging among their respective political affinity groups. If you create art that has an ethical, political, or cultural bent, be sure to emphasize it to deepen this connection.

Esteem

Luxury cars, watches, jewelry, fashionable clothes, lifestyle products, furniture, and more fulfill people's social-status-related esteem needs. In the abundant artist lessons, we talked about how luxury buyers are suspicious when a price is too low. However, a better reason to set prices high is that paying the higher price helps satisfy the buyer's need for esteem. There's something called a Veblen good (named after economist Thorstein Veblen). Basically, a Veblen good is a luxury item that, when its price increases, demand also increases. Rolex watches and Veuve Clicquot would be considered Veblen goods. They're generally quality products whose demand increases with price, as they're considered status symbols.[4] Similarly, designer clothing sells better *because* of its high prices, not despite them. Designer fashion buyers (and all luxury buyers) want the items because a price tag that relatively few people can afford makes the item exclusive. Teslas are an example of a luxury good that is both a Veblen good and satisfies the conscious consumer's need to shop their values. Buyers of Teslas are letting the world know that sustainability matters to them, and also that they have the means to drop six figures on an electric car. When you're pricing your art, remember that the higher price tag will attract the high-end buyers who are craving exclusivity.

Self-Actualization

Maslow described self-actualization as the desire to reach our full potential. If you're selling classes, you want to speak to a person's personal growth and self-fulfillment. And, of course, creative makers who sell art, such as jewelry, clothing, and decorative art, help people see themselves as living their best life. More subtle connection points may also include how the person views their character, not just adorning their physical appearance and environment. For example, Michelle Obama donned a "vote" necklace at the 2020 Democratic National Convention, encouraging people to do just that: have a say and vote. Women who wanted to express their political empowerment made this one of the bestselling pieces for byChari.com, an independent, Black-owned, female-led jewelry business founded by Chari Cuthbert.[5] Once, I sold a $400 original painting of a pig to a woman to give as a gift to her pig-obsessed niece even though the price tag exceeded her initial gift budget. By helping my customer see herself as the kind of aunt who dotes on her relatives with arts and culture, I allowed her to feel good about spending money. What people really want to buy is a better version of themselves and their lives. This isn't about manipulating customers; your goal is to help them recognize their core desires and see how your art helps them fulfill those longings.

WORDS THAT SELL

Whether you're selling online or in person, your choice of words can help your prospects see how your product or service gets them to that better version of themselves. Selling online, many artists imagine they need to use flowery language to describe their products and services. Others who dislike writing or believe "awesome" art will sell itself sometimes resort to slapping a price on their art and calling it a day. You don't have to go to either extreme. When writing copy for your website or sales emails, talk about your art from the heart and tell stories about why you created it. When you're selling your art in person, let your buyer do most of the talking and ask guiding questions to help them decide.

Include as many of these positive words and phrases as you can in the marketing copy on your website and in your emails, in talking to prospects, or wherever you sell your art. In addition to sprinkling in power words, you'll also want to avoid words that have a negative connotation.

POWER WORDS AND PHRASES	WHY TO USE THEM
Safe, Easy, Trust, Proven, Has you covered, Guaranteed, No risk, Cancel at any time, Free demo, See for yourself	Numerous studies have shown that humans avoid risk. Demonstrating the ways you have minimized risk helps convert sales. All these words and phrases help your customer feel at ease. Our fear-based brains are repelled by risk, so these words put our minds at ease. Example: packed safely.
Save	It's helpful to sprinkle in this word, whether your product saves time, money, or embarrassment.
Love	Using emotion words in marketing is very powerful,[6] and the word "love" is the most positive. Example: easy to love this art.
Money, Value	Words that indicate that the customer will save money or get a good value will influence the sale.
New, Best	These types of words demonstrate value and also satisfy the human desire for esteem since they are getting products first.
Discover, Own	Action verbs motivate people to take action.
You	Your marketing copy should always be about them and how they will benefit—not you. Using the word "you" is a great placeholder for their name.
Imagine	When you mentally rehearse your prospects to imagine the pleasure they'll derive from owning your product, you increase the likelihood that they'll purchase. This process is also known as "future pacing."

Exclusive, Limited, Made for you	Remind your prospects that your item is either one of a kind or part of a limited edition. Personalization can also make the customer feel special (and appeals to their need for belonging!).
Because	This word satisfies the brain's need for reasons.

Here's a short list of negative words to watch out for and words you can use instead, but you can also get creative. For example, instead of using the word "buy," animal artists can use the phrase "Would you like to *adopt* this painting?"

WORDS TO AVOID	TRY THIS INSTEAD
Buy	Collect, Own, Invest, Add, Adopt
Contract	Paperwork, Agreement
Cost or Price	Value, Investment, Range, Available for
Customer	Client, Collector, Friend, Patron, Student
Deal	Opportunity
Down payment or Deposit	Initial investment
Sell or Selling	Exhibit, Offer, Show
Sign	Approve, Endorse, Complete paperwork

WHAT ARTPRENEURS NEED TO BELIEVE

- As artists, we can use emotion to sell our art.
- If you're focused only on how your art solves a problem, you're focused on the lowest value your art can provide.
- Paying higher prices helps satisfy the buyer's need for esteem.

MARCHING ORDERS

- Tweak your offerings and the way you talk about them to trigger positive buying psychology.
- Treat interactions with prospects as you would a conversation with a close friend, sharing honestly and authentically.
- Help your customers recognize their core desires and see how your art helps them fulfill those longings.

"WHEN PEOPLE TALK,
LISTEN COMPLETELY.
MOST PEOPLE NEVER
LISTEN."

—ERNEST HEMINGWAY

LISTEN TO UNDERSTAND

MANY ARTISTS BELIEVE YOU MUST be extroverted or have the "right" personality to be good at sales. The truth is selling is a *skill*—and anyone can do it, even if you're more reserved. Shy people and introverts are often good listeners, and listening is the number-one skill you need for selling. When selling in person, you're speaking to one person at a time, and your ability to listen is far more important than, say, being witty. (I'm so animated on my podcast that most people are surprised to learn that I'm shy and consider myself an introvert. Podcasting is a great way to become "famous" without ever having to leave your home!) If you're worried about what to say in a sales conversation, you can relax since most of these steps involve *listening* to your customers and making them feel comfortable. In addition, with a sales process, you won't have to worry about relying on your personality to sell.

• • •

ARTPRENEUR SALES PLAYBOOK: TEN STEPS FOR SELLING

I'm going to walk you through the ten steps for selling. In my examples, I'll be emphasizing in-person selling. Remember that online selling is just a virtual version of what happens in person. Once you understand and master the nuances of in-person sales, you'll be able to apply this process to the online world easily.

Step One: Introduce Yourself

Establishing trust starts with making your buyers feel comfortable. When I'm selling in person, one of the first things I do when someone enters my space is introduce myself. This is part of Social Skills 101, but then I'm always surprised by how few salespeople tell me who they are or ask for my name. I'm thinking, "Who are you? You're trying to sell to me, but I don't even know your name." (On the flip side, when I'm shopping or at a restaurant and want better service, often I'll introduce myself and ask for the clerk's or server's name.) Make it your objective to treat everyone you meet as you would a guest at your party and show them love and affection (of course, not in a creepy way). When you show people you like them, they're more likely to feel welcome and reciprocate those feelings, which creates a stronger connection.

The introduction is simple. For example, I'll say, "Hey, I'm Miriam, and I'm the artist. What's your name?" (Otherwise, I may have to correct customers who assume that my assistant with the blue hair and a nose ring is the artist and that I'm her mother.) In addition, wearing a name tag makes you more accessible and helps people remember your name. I also like to carry a clipboard so I can write down their names right away and later refer to my prospects by name. This clipboard also holds my sales slips, and the email collection cards we talked about in chapter 8.

Step Two: Chitchat

Most shy people either avoid or rush through small talk because we get anxious about what's to come. But breaking the ice in a friendly, non-salesy manner relaxes your buyers and puts them at ease.

One of my most successful art-selling venues for over twelve years was the holiday boutique at the music school where my daughter took lessons. Now, at an event where most vendors sell items like handbags and jewelry, you wouldn't think a fine artist would do well; yet I consistently outsold all the other vendors, year after year—and small talk helped. When I introduced myself to the music moms and dads, I might first ask, "What instrument does your kid play?" Then I add, "My daughter took lessons here." I created a connection before we ever talk about my art, warming up a stranger in a matter of seconds.

At other events, I might say to browsers, "Oh, do you live here?" or "Did you come here from out of town?" You might even talk about the weather. Just chit-chatty things. Initiating small talk engenders trust. If you try to rush into other sales techniques before you've established rapport, it can be very off-putting for your prospect. Even if you're visiting your prospect's home, it's still best to start with an icebreaker.

Never start by asking them, "How can I help you?" That's the fastest way to scare away a customer! What they hear is: "Can I sell to you now?" Their knee-jerk response will always be negative—usually some version of "I'm good. I'm just looking." Or "There's no room on my walls." Connecting through small talk keeps them from putting up defenses.

+ + + **VIRTUAL VERSION** + + +

When you're talking with people in DMs, be a human, and for Pete's sake do *not* code a bot to do this for you. Nothing turns off a prospect faster than getting an automated message—and we can all tell when it's not real. In addition, each message needs to ask permission to take the next step in the conversation. I can't stand it when marketers send me a three-paragraph DM, usually sent by their assistant, pitching me on their products or webinars. You don't need to give your prospect all that information in one long message. For your prospect, this is the equivalent of walking into a department store and getting sprayed by perfume. Allow conversations to evolve naturally using an authentic back-and-forth process as you respond to what they're saying in real time.

Step Three: Slip in a Credibility Marker

Next, ask a planned rhetorical question that includes a credibility marker. A credibility marker shows that you're legit. Let's say you got some great press with your photo in the local paper. Instead of breaking the ice by asking, "How did you find me?" or "How did you find out about this event?"—ask, "Are you here because you saw my article in *Greenwich Time*?" You can also work in your credentials later in the sales conversation. You might say something like, "Oh, you probably read on my website that Beyoncé collects my art." Or you might say, "I'm feeling a little tired right now because I've been working overtime to finish an installation for Jennifer Lopez." I'm *not* suggesting you make things up. Insert whatever credibility markers are true for you.

+ + + **VIRTUAL VERSION** + + +

When I introduce myself to new Instagram followers, I ask them if they found me through my podcast, *The Inspiration Place*. Many of my new followers haven't found my podcast yet, and that's a great way to let them know I have one. If you have a blog or a YouTube channel that you want your followers to know about, you can ask them about that or if perhaps they found you because of a recent press opportunity.

Step Four: Ask Leading Questions

After the necessary initial chitchat, ask more leading questions to understand what your prospects want, and why. Telling isn't selling, so the more you listen to your customer, the more successful you'll be. When people engage in my artwork, my go-to questions are: "What kinds of art do you collect?" or "Do you prefer to collect prints or originals?" Asking such questions helps you establish what they want without asking them the dreaded "What are you looking for?" Binary questions are easier to answer than open-ended ones, and some can still provide you great information. For example, you can ask, "Are you looking for yourself or a gift?"

Ask questions that provoke your client's emotions and tap into their psychology. For example, when I sold the pig painting to the aunt who fashioned herself as a real-life Auntie Mame, I phrased my statement as a question using a tie-down. I asked, "You want to be the kind of aunt who treats their niece to original art, is that right?" Tie-downs are phrases that can turn any statement into a question; so, for example, if you catch yourself *telling* your customer (when you should be asking), you can always tack on a "Don't you agree?" at the end. If your suggestion isn't what they have in mind, you'll want to figure out why so you can lead them to something different.

Bad salespeople believe selling looks like this: "This is what I'm selling. It costs $X. Let me convince you now. Blah blah blah. Do you want to buy it?" They talk about their product and tell their customers how they should feel about it. Again, telling isn't selling. (After all, no one wants to go to a party and have someone talk at them all night. Most people prefer to be listened to.) Instead, draft a list of questions that lead your prospects to describe what they want. With this process, you can help them figure out why what you have is what they desire.

Keep following up with clarifying questions. You're not questioning just to ask questions. You're asking to lead them to something in your selling space or on your website that they would like (or, perhaps, to discover that what you offer isn't for them after all—and that saves you time and effort). Once you've asked enough questions to understand them better, you might ask, "Is this similar to what you have in mind?"

In active listening, don't interrupt your customer. I know this can be challenging if you get excited when you talk about your art. If you're worried about forgetting what you want to ask them next, you can take notes during this conversation and write down your next question. Make sure to keep your mouth closed while you're listening, so you don't look like you're about to say anything. This encourages them to keep talking. You're listening to understand, so it doesn't even matter if you forget what you wanted to say next. Making sales isn't about what you say—it's always about listening. Hopefully, knowing that your role is mostly to listen and ask questions while they do the talking will take the pressure off.

Step Five: Mind Your Body Language

When selling in person, body language matters. Don't be that artist sitting in the corner with a cup of coffee. Plan for a long day on your feet. When you stand and meet customers at eye level, you'll project confidence and come across as more engaging. (Some artists invest in directors' chairs so that they can be seated and still meet customers who come into their space at eye level.) On the other hand, don't hover over prospects, as that could make you seem desperate and creepy. Most people will maintain a social distance that feels comfortable to them, but a good rule of thumb is four feet apart. However, if a customer takes a step back, recognize their social distance may be greater than yours, especially given our years of social distancing for health reasons (or it could be your coffee breath). Plan something for busying yourself inside your selling space while remaining engaged. Some examples include adding pricing stickers to new inventory or rearranging your display table. These busy activities should never be so engrossing, such as engaging with your phone, that they might make your prospects feel you're too busy for them. That's why I don't do live painting demonstrations in my booth when I'm trying to sell.

Step Six: Preview the Process to Make Prospects Comfortable

When beginning a formal sales call, such as a home visit or a video consultation, outline the process of the sales call for your customer. These previews work for selling both commissioned artwork and services.

In a commission situation, you might tell your customer, "I'm going to ask you questions about what you want to have commissioned, and then we'll discuss color and sizes. I'll answer questions you might have and explain the process." When you're selling a service, you might begin with small talk, and then say, "First, I'm going to ask you questions about your goals. Then, if it makes sense, we can talk about how you would work with me." In both cases, you're outlining the process, so they know what to expect. Letting customers know the structure of the sales call puts them at ease. The human brain doesn't like uncertainty, and people who are uncomfortable or confused aren't going to buy. So, whenever you're selling, make sure you prioritize your customers' comfort and clarity.

Step Seven: Establish The Decision-Maker

When selling in person at art festivals, boutiques, or brick-and-mortar shops, you'll get a lot of looky-loos or window shoppers. (Heck, you'll also get plenty of tire kickers online!) Some browsers feel empowered to make buying decisions on their own, and others won't want to make a purchase without a second opinion. The latter type of buyer may offer this information right away. ("Hey, I don't buy art without my wife.") If the decision requires a second person, you'll want to know that up front. For example, you don't want to book an appointment with just the wife, only to hear her say, "I have to ask my husband," or vice versa. You want to make sure both decision-makers are present.

Sometimes looping in a second opinion helps close sales. For example, if the husband who only buys art with his wife happens to stumble across an artwork he loves, you can offer to let him email a photo to her. I've had customers send pictures to their partners or to interior decorators. My client Linda (whom you met in chapter 5) shared with me that once she had a husband Face-Time with his wife, so not only could she see the artwork, but Linda could also engage with her. When both partners are engaged in the process, it usually leads to a happy ending. (And don't be afraid someone will copy or pirate your work by taking a photo. If people are asking to take pictures, ask them to tag you on social media so you can benefit from the free publicity.)

When I have a portrait commission, I make sure to book the important milestones of the process with all decision-makers present. For this process, I take photographs of the kids, and we hold a session to choose the photos. I always make sure both partners are there. Otherwise, I'm wasting my time, because there's no guarantee that the partners will agree on the photo to use. Also, with both parties there, I'm on hand to help them make that decision together. Unless you're creating a surprise gift, you want to make sure all key decision-makers are present.

+ + + **VIRTUAL VERSION** + + +

When you book videoconferences, ensure all the right people are on the call. If you need both decision-makers and only one is present, you'll have to rely on one of them to be a good salesperson for you.

Step Eight: Sell with Stories

At my very first outdoor art show, my display was positioned directly across from a cotton-candy-haired artist wearing a seafoam green polyester pantsuit. Her pedestrian watercolors of flowers and beach scenes didn't stand out as being better than the other artwork at this show, yet she made significantly more sales than the rest of us that day. I had to discover her secret, so I asked. She generously shared, "I never tell them I painted this in my studio from a photo. Instead, I might say that it was such a hot day. I got a sunburn, and I was mesmerized by the ocean and the children playing in the surf." Short stories that paint a picture and conjure up emotions and sensations are especially effective.

When a collector asks about a piece, they're looking for a story, not a description of your technique or process. Even when a prospect asks, "How long does it take you to make your art?" they're not really looking for information about how many hours it took. (Many artists are offended when people ask that, but I can promise you that customers aren't trying to calculate your hourly wage.) Most often they're asking that because they want to talk to you about your art, but don't know what to ask. Consider a question like that an invitation to tell a story. But if you have a story to share about your art, always get permission from the prospect to tell it. For example, you can say, "I have a story about that. Would you like to hear it?" Or "Would you like to know my inspiration?" The story behind the art or why you became an artist helps people connect with your art, which often leads to a sale.

Whenever possible, though, you'll want to hear your customers' stories before sharing your own. Venezuelan abstract painter Marisabel Gonzalez shared that when someone is staring at her art, she doesn't launch into stories. Instead, she asks, "How does this make you feel? What drew you to this piece?" If someone is staring at your art, they're clearly making a connection and creating their own story. To sell your art, invite them to share. People are drawn to your art because of what it means to them—and sometimes people will project their own stories on your creations. Draw out those stories, because they're how people convince themselves to buy your art. Buyers want their own fantasy of what you're offering. They're buying what's in their imagination, not the facts.

Cindy Mawle, who paints landscapes of the Pacific Northwest, shared with me why she doesn't like to reveal the exact locations of her landscapes. She said, "You have to be careful because they may have something in their head of what that painting is. If you suddenly say, 'Oh no, that's a painting of such and such thing,' you might burst their bubble and lose sales that way."[1] Instead, she asks them what the place reminds them of, unless they insist on knowing the exact place.

Kindra Hall, the author of *Stories That Stick*, told me that stories drive her art-collecting habits. "I'm not buying just the piece of art. I'm buying the story that I'm going to talk about that art when someone comes over to my house."[2]

Hall suggested that the best way to get prospects to disclose their own stories is to share a short story of your own. She explained, "What you're really doing is saying, 'This is a storytelling environment here.'" She added, "Every story you tell is an opportunity for someone to tell a story back to you. Stories beget stories." She also suggested that the stories you receive from prospects and customers will enhance your own messaging.

+ + + **VIRTUAL VERSION** + + +

Social media provides a place to practice telling short stories and seeing what the response is. Some of my best posts are the ones that start with "True story." Then I tell a story that might be related to what I created. Those same stories end up in my emails and on my website. My art collectors are reluctant to collect the art if there's no story on my website. I've had collectors tell me they like the piece, but they wonder, "What's the story?"

Just as you would in person, create space online for people to project their own feelings. I never tell people, "This painting is meant to make you feel happy." Instead, tell a story about it and then ask, "How does it make you feel?" In the end, people don't buy the story; they buy the emotions they feel in response to your narrative.

Step Nine: Overcome Objections

A wonderful benefit of connecting with your customers emotionally is that they overcome their own objections to buying and talk themselves into a purchase. Hearing an objection isn't a bad thing. It means you're close to making a sale. (Remember, customers' brains are offering up reasons to avoid risk.) Often you can overcome objections by telling stories and asking questions. (An overcoming objections chart is included at the end of this section.) Share stories about other customers who had the same concern and how it worked out well for them. For example, parents with several children usually have stacks of photos where one child has his or her eyes closed, or another sibling didn't quite cooperate in the moment. These parents fear my painting will reflect those unsuccessful photos. That's why I share stories about triple portraits and how I usually combine multiple photos—since in any one photo it's common for one sibling to have been acting out. Parents with more than one child can fully relate to that experience, and that promotes trust. It's even better when you can share a specific story that illustrates your point.

Of course, there are many other objections you might hear from customers. Copywriter Danielle Weil says, "What I like to do with my clients is an exercise of thinking through and making a list of all of the things that your ideal customer, student, client needs to believe in order to buy."[3] Here's an example of how I overcome objections when selling portraits. My clients are afraid of not liking the result. They need to believe I can create a portrait that looks like the person they want painted. I always have a lot of photos of both the subject and my finished portraits so they can see that I've captured a likeness. This way if a customer is hesitating because they're worried whether I can create a likeness, they have lots of examples of happy endings. That's why businesses focus effort on gathering testimonials from satisfied customers and before-and-after photos. You can do this, too, by asking your customers for feedback after they have purchased, and make sure their stories are posted on your website, social media, and other promotional materials.

+ + + VIRTUAL VERSION + + +

When I'm selling art classes, my students need to believe they can paint in watercolor, which is why I share lots of stories (and pictures) from students who were also intimidated but happy with their results. In addition, both my art students and my collectors need to believe the process is going to be emotionally rewarding. Once you make a list of potential objections, you can answer them through the copy on your website—or with the words you say through conversations with your prospects—in a way that feels natural. No flowery language required.

About the sales process, copywriter Weil said, "The way that I like to talk about it is talking about a bridge that you're taking someone across. On one side of the bridge is someone whipping out their credit card and going, 'Yes, please take my money.' On the other side of the bridge are those people, your ideal collectors, your ideal people waiting over there for you to take them across. And it's your job, with the words that you use, to build that bridge for them and make it really, really easy for them to walk across." When you listen to your customers and understand their core desires, writing your copy will become easier.

Limit buyers' choices. Recently, I needed a sports bra and headed over to the online athleisure store Athleta. When I typed in "sports bra," over 530 items came up in myriad shapes, sizes, and colors, which didn't make my buying process easier. Instead, the site overwhelmed me with too many options. Remember we talked about decision drama in chapter 4? Your customers don't like making decisions either. Many artists believe they should put everything out "just in case." However, a curated selection yields more sales. If you're getting a lot of "I'll think about it," ask yourself whether you gave your customers too many choices.

Create urgency. If you've curated your selections and your customers are still telling you they need to think about it, give them a deadline or a reason to decide by a specific date. For example, you can offer free shipping if they purchase before the deadline. I only offer discounts if their objection also involves price. For example, a woman at one of my in-person events was spending a long time trying to decide between three prints, so I asked, "Why don't you get all three?" In this case, she wasn't sure she wanted to *pay* for three, so I told her, "If you purchase all three, I'll give you 10 percent off." With a smile, she pulled out her credit card and bought them all. If she had told me she wasn't sure which would look best in her home, I might've offered her free returns instead.

Project confidence. You might also get lots of "I'll think about it" if you're projecting uncertainty. Customers can sniff out your self-doubt and will then have trouble trusting you. Remember that to sell more art, you've got to be sold on yourself. Doing the thought work we've discussed throughout the book helps you manage your mind and project confidence. And when you honor your own commitments, you'll build that confidence naturally. That's what we'll be talking about in the next chapter.

+ + + **VIRTUAL VERSION** + + +

When you're selling at an in-person event, there's a natural urgency because customers realize that it's a unique experience that ends soon. Online, there's a sense that your products will always be available, so you must give customers a firm deadline to act. Some sellers believe the more time we give someone to think about it, the more likely they'll be to buy. Unfortunately, the more time customers have, the more likely they'll be to come up with reasons not to buy. Again, whenever the brain senses risk, it naturally comes up with all the reasons why doing that risky, scary thing is a bad idea. That's why it's best to urge your customers to decide quickly by imposing a deadline. Rather than being manipulative, you're helping them make up their minds. People don't like the feeling of indecision, so you're doing them a favor by encouraging them to decide.

Now I want to walk you through some of the best strategies for handling objections with the following chart. Notice how the best way to handle them is by asking questions that help buyers see that their thoughts are optional. Listen carefully to your customers and make it safe for your customer to say no to you. The goal is not to get a "yes" at any cost or to convince them to do something they don't want to do, but to help your customers feel safe to say yes.

Overcoming Objections: Action Steps and Scripts

Objection	"I need to think about it" or "I want to think it over …"
Potential Rationale Behind Their Objection	What's happening here is that your art collector is feeling uncomfortable about the amount of money that they're about to spend, and they want to "think about it" because they're hoping that it will make them feel more comfortable. However, that's a thought that usually isn't true. Meaning the way they feel about making a decision won't change with time. Usually giving your customer more time to think about it gives them time to come up with unhelpful stories about why it's a bad idea.
Inspired Action Steps and Scripts	Make sure your choices are curated to alleviate decision overwhelm. Tell them, "That's a great idea," and put the item back on the shelf (or on the wall). Sometimes, removing the item from them creates a sense of loss and they will then want to own it. Give the customer a deadline and an incentive to buy before the deadline (such as free shipping, a percentage off, or a bonus). Remind them that you offer returns.

Objection	"I have to ask my _____." (partner/interior decorator, mother, etc.)
Potential Rationale Behind Their Objection	Making decisions is difficult, and your customer is afraid of making a mistake.
Inspired Action Steps and Scripts	**Action Steps:** Offer to let them send a picture to the other decision-maker. Offer them a money-back guarantee if the other decision-maker doesn't like it, or offer to let them "try before they buy." **Scripts:** "Are you a 'yes' if they are a 'no'?" "What do you hope they will say?" "What will you do if they say no?" "Is this decision dependent on their approval?"

Objection	"It's too expensive."
Potential Rationale Behind Their Objection	Your customer may have money mindset issues. Don't take this to mean that your art is too expensive. They may have never invested this kind of money before. Sometimes they present a money objection when that isn't their only concern (or it isn't the true concern). That's why asking these other questions will help uncover their true objection, which may be easily addressed. When they express money concerns and you agree with them, you can help normalize their uncomfortable feelings. You can make spending that kind of money aspirational.

Agree with your customer.

Ask them their budget and guide them to an item with a price that is closer to what they had in mind.

Scripts:

"Is the price your only concern?"

"Is there something else?"

"How far apart are we?" (If you're willing to negotiate.)

"If you collect all three, I'll give you 10 percent off."

"Do you agree with the value of this?"

"Have you ever spent money like this before on art?" If they say yes, you can ask them about what it was they invested in and how they felt about it. If they say no, you can say, "It makes sense that spending that kind of money makes you feel uncomfortable, *and it's normal to feel this way.*" Follow up by asking, "Is there an amount you would have felt good saying yes to?"

"I can't afford it."

They choose not to pay for what you have, or they have money mindset issues.

Scripts:
"What does that mean to you?"

"Did you come here today expecting to collect art?"

"What did you ballpark this to be?"

"Do you think the price is fair?"

Objection	"I'm saving up for it."
Potential Rationale Behind Their Objection	They're trying to delay making this decision.
Inspired Action Steps and Scripts	An effective strategy is to allow them to make a deposit to hold the artwork and work out a payment plan. This strategy is particularly effective when the art is a one-of-a-kind original and the customer would "miss out" on it. **Ask them:** "Is this what you do for most big purchases?" "What trade-off will you have to make to save for this?" "Is there anything that could bump this as a priority?"

Objection	"I'm just shopping around."
Potential Rationale Behind Their Objection	This is FOMO (fear of missing out), or looking for bigger, better things. Sometimes people don't even have a process for making a decision, and these questions will help reveal that to your customer.
Inspired Action Steps and Scripts	**Ask them:** "When will you know you've found the _____ (right art)?" "What criteria are you using?" "Have you defined what you're looking for?" "If you had to decide yes or no right now, what would the answer be?"

Step Ten: Close the Sale

As you move your prospects closer to the sale, they may ask questions that signal they're ready to buy. For example, if they ask about payment, that's generally a good sign. However, for times when you're not sure whether you're getting close to a sale, "test-close" questions come in handy. "Where do you imagine displaying this in your home?" and "Is this for yourself or is it a gift?" are good test-close questions. After those questions, you can start using presumptive language, such as "How would you like to pay?" If you ask these questions too early and they back-fire, you can return to overcoming their objections.

When you're selling in person, make sure you have an electronic means for accepting credit cards. This is easier than ever with a device that syncs to an app on your cell phone or tablet or having an app such as PayPal, Venmo, Zelle, or Apple Pay or a link to your e-commerce-enabled website such as Shopify or Squarespace. Many artists now put QR codes directly on their price tags so that customers can sync up checkout with their smartphones. You'll make larger sales when you're able to accept credit cards or electronic payments as well as cash or checks.

+ + + **VIRTUAL VERSION** + + +

Make it easy for customers to buy. That sounds so obvious, but many artists are missing a way for customers to check out. Yes, you need prices on your website with a button for people to check out electronically. And you need a shopping cart embedded on your website. Once, I was admiring an artist's printed tea towels on Instagram. She instructed me to DM her so she could email me pictures of the five choices she offered, since she didn't have a website. Later, she complained that even though she received many compliments, people didn't want to buy her towels. She thought it was because her prices were too high. In truth, her prices were too high for the *inconvenience.*

Lacking a user-friendly means for customers to make a purchase makes you look unprofessional and annoys your potential customers. Imagine Pottery Barn sending you a postcard with a picture of one tea towel and instructions to call them so they could email you more pictures. Make the shopping process easy and delightful, and you'll have more sales.

+ + + **MINDSET CHECK-IN** + + +

What's coming up for you? Write down all your fears and doubts about asking for the sale. Are you afraid of sounding salesy? Are you worried that you'll hear a "no"?

Label your thought distortions:

Mind reading = MR | Fortune-telling = FT
All-or-nothing thinking = AON

Notice which thoughts aren't serving you.

WHAT ARTPRENEURS NEED TO BELIEVE

- When you show people that you like them, they're more likely to feel welcome and reciprocate those feelings, which builds a stronger connection.
- The story behind the art or your journey as an artist helps people connect with your art, which often leads to a sale.

MARCHING ORDERS

- Break the ice in a friendly, non-salesy manner to put your buyer at ease.
- Make clarity and your prospects' comfort high priorities.
- Connect with customers emotionally to help them overcome their own objections and talk themselves into making a purchase.

"YOU HAVE TO KNOW WHAT YOU WANT TO GET IT."

—GERTRUDE STEIN

STAY INSPIRED

TWIRLING HER HAIR AROUND A FINGER, Margaret sighed. "I procrastinate because I lack self-confidence. If only I were more confident, I wouldn't do that." Margaret shared this with me during our consultation. I think she expected me to agree and tell her my coaching program would fix her confidence so she wouldn't procrastinate anymore. She was a little surprised when I contradicted her.

"Actually. You lack confidence *because* you procrastinate. Each time you don't do what you say you're going to do, you erode your self-trust."

She paused for a moment, staring at a point out in space. "Yes. I think you're right. So how do I fix that?"

Many artists believe they lack confidence because of their poor results. They think that if they had better results, such as more sales, they would gain more confidence. Others, such as Margaret, think the reason they're procrastinating and not focusing is due to the same lack of confidence. They don't yet know that the secret to unlocking greater confidence lies in your ability to learn to trust yourself, and that starts with following through on your commitments.

You won't always be in control of your results, but you're always in control of the actions you take. You're also in control of the thoughts and feelings that drive those actions. When you manage your mind to produce thoughts and feelings that inspire you, you're taking what I call inspired action. And when you consistently take inspired action, your confidence soars, and the results you seek become inevitable.

During my first year of college, I signed up for an honors physics class. This was a big mistake. I figured I was always good at math (dating back to my fraction talent), but I was inadequately prepared for the college-level curriculum. Many of my classmates already had many physics courses under their belts. But lack of preparation for honors physics wasn't my only challenge; I failed the first physics test and wasn't performing much better in my other classes.

I looked around at classmates who I knew were popping No-Doz, and I wondered if I just wasn't working hard enough. Fortunately, my physics professor had noticed the many careless errors on my test, such as transposing numbers—a red flag. As a result, he recommended me for academic testing to rule out dyslexia or another learning challenge.

After a series of assessments, the results showed that I have auditory processing disorder, a learning difference not unlike dyslexia. Although there's no medication or treatment course to "fix" a processing disorder, my college's Academic Skills Center recommended that I take advantage of their resources to learn better study techniques. The school also granted me extra accommodations to manage my test anxiety; however, the skill I learned that made the biggest difference, and which I still use today, is *creating a schedule.*

Before I dive into the particulars of this process, I wanted to take a moment to point out that I've always considered the way

I think to be an asset rather than a disability. I've never regarded my own neurodiversity and divergent thinking as disadvantages. I consider them to be two of my greatest strengths in building a business. My impulsivity enables me to hesitate less when taking risks and to make quicker decisions. My distractibility makes it easier for me to come up with fresh, outside-the-box ideas. And, finally, although I process auditory stimulation differently, that difference also allows me to think in an artistic way.

Since music, visual arts, crafts, and dance give students with learning differences a chance to express themselves through different media, many people with learning differences find joy and confidence through the arts. As a result, there are often many people within the arts community who have learning differences, such as ADHD, dyslexia, autism, and a host of other neurodiverse features. If this is you, know that the very things that may challenge you in some areas of your life can also be your superpower as an artpreneur.

One of the most valuable things you'll learn from this book is how to manage your priorities and your schedule to reach your goals. Many productivity programs focus on getting more tasks done without considering whether you're even doing the *right* things. In this productivity system, you'll learn how to set goals and then manage your priorities so that you're focusing your valuable time (and energy) on the five foundations of the Passion-to-Profit framework—which ensures that you're doing what matters most. You'll also learn how to continuously reactivate your inspiration so you're acting from the energy of positive motivation rather than pushing past negative doubts.

GOAL GETTING (NOT JUST SETTING)

Effective time management is about getting clear on your goals, your priorities, and how you spend your day. Many people set New Year's resolutions, which isn't the same as goal setting.

According to a 2007 survey of over three thousand people conducted by the British psychologist Richard Wiseman, 88 percent of participants failed to keep their resolutions.[1] There's a better way. Instead of creating New Year's resolutions, create goals. You don't have to wait for an arbitrary starting point, like the beginning of a new calendar year, to reimagine your future.

Unfortunately, many people haven't even *thought* of any specific goals, let alone shared them. When I ask artists what their goals are, they sometimes murmur something vague about wanting to "get their art out there." If you don't have a vision for your future, you aren't going to have the grit or the commitment to make any kind of progress. Not having a goal is like getting in your car and driving aimlessly until you run out of gas. To make any progress, you need to know where you're going and how you're going to get there.

I THINK A LOT OF PEOPLE DREAM. AND WHILE THEY ARE BUSY DREAMING, THE REALLY HAPPY PEOPLE, THE REALLY SUCCESSFUL PEOPLE, THE REALLY INTERESTING, ENGAGED, POWERFUL PEOPLE, ARE BUSY DOING.

—SHONDA RHIMES

Making it as an artpreneur requires three key components: a destination, a strategy for getting there, and a method for tracking progress. Setting goals will give you a clear destination for planning your days and weeks. Your strategy consists of the steps you'll take to support production, prospecting, and promotion. Finally, you need to track your progress to make sure your strategy is moving you closer to your destination.

Here's my signature seven-step process for goal achievement.

Step One: Write Down Your Goals

Do you write down your goals on a regular basis? Or do you simply think about them without documenting them? According to a study by psychology professor Dr. Gail Matthews, you're 42 percent more likely to achieve your goals simply by writing them down on a regular basis.[2] Imagination and writing occur on opposite sides of your brain. Imagination happens on the right side of the brain, but when we write, our logical left brain takes over. This approach creates a whole-mind awareness of your goals, putting your brain to work to find ways to help you achieve them. Your brain will continue to search for inspired actions to move you closer to your goals.

Brainstorm in a journal. I often begin a goal-setting session by brainstorming my desires in an art journal, making large, pretty bubble letters. As I spend time coloring in these personal and business goals, I'm meditating on them. Of course, you don't need to create art journal pages as part of your own goal-setting process. Regular writing works fine—and your mind-body connection will be stronger when you write. Writing activates the reticular processing center of your brain.[3] This is the part of your brain that helps you process and focus. As a result, the physical act of writing as you brainstorm brings the information to the forefront and triggers your brain to pay close attention. Moreover, writing engages more of your senses than just thinking about it. When you write, you're using your sense of touch and sight.

Create categories for your goals. Many people's categories include love, health, creativity, work, family, friends, community, and religion or spirituality, but your own categories can be anything. (For example, though I sell my art to make money, I separate my creative goals from my income goals, because not all the art I create needs to be monetized.) Use whatever categories and words make sense for you. Plus, have your goals balanced in more than one area. For example, maybe you'll want a health goal, an income goal, a personal development or spiritual goal, and a creative or intellectual goal. If you don't balance your goals, you may overfocus on your career and let your relationships suffer.

But whatever you choose as your categories, keep in mind that to support your aim to make it as an artist, you'll need at least three goals: for your production (creating your art), your prospecting (building your audience), and promotion (selling). Taking the actions to meet these primary goals will be essential to your success.

In contemplating everything you want, don't concern yourself with whether the goals are realistic. Just allow your mind to wander and daydream. List everything you want without judgment or editing. You can edit these goals in the steps that follow. Next, select only the ones most important to you for the set time period, whether that's a year or less. Don't assign yourself too many goals at once: certainly, no more than ten for the year—and preferably quite a bit fewer. If you chase too many priorities, you'll end up splitting your focus and feeling scattered. As you make your plan to take inspired action, continue to drill down, eliminating the fluff and focusing on the essential elements.

Make it specific and measurable. When you're setting your goals, make each one specific—including a deadline for completion. For example, a specific creative goal might be to create three collections for the year. Vague goals, such as "This year I'm going to paint more," may suffice for New Year's resolutions, but they don't work at all well for accomplishing anything. With a specific destination, you'll always know how much progress you're making. Tracking progress is a key step in the goal-getting process. (We'll get there in a moment.) Make sure each goal is measurable. Making your goals both specific and measurable enables you to keep yourself accountable for your results, and to achieve the success you're dreaming of.

Dream big. You're not going to go any further than your dream, so dream big. If your dream is too small, it will limit you. That's why, when you're brainstorming, it's not helpful to think about what's realistic. Often, we set goals that are too small because we fear disappointing ourselves. An example of a small goal would be selling enough to cover the cost of your art supplies or making some side-hustle money. If your dreams only see your art business as a hobby, earning hobby money, then you won't grow beyond that. What income would replace your day job? What kind of success would give you the lifestyle you want? Start there. Revisit the belief triad and imagine limitless possibilities for yourself. If you believe in yourself, your art, and the audience out there waiting for you to show up, what do you *then* imagine? Set a "goal beyond the goal"—a stretch goal. Shoot for the stars with a big vision.

Set an income goal for yourself, a number that stretches beyond your comfort zone. But also think about your goals that aren't income specific but that satisfy one of the pillars of the Passion-to-Profit framework. Start with your production plan. What do you want to create this year? Next, create a prospecting goal, such as growing your list of email subscribers by one thousand people. And set a promotion goal. Plan, say, six to twelve promotions per year to sell your products and services. Remember that you'll need to link your production efforts with your income goals, as discussed in chapter 5. If your aim is to make $60,000 for the year and you plan to run six promotions, to reach that goal you need to create at least $10,000 in inventory for each promotion. Finally, create a plan for original content that supports your prospecting and promotion efforts.

Stay in an abundance mindset. When focusing on all the things you want but don't yet have, you might find yourself slipping into a scarcity mindset. Here's a way to counter that. To your list of things that you want, also add the things you want that you *already have*. For example, I might say I want a healthy son and a daughter, and I already have both. By recognizing that you already have some of the things you want, you'll spark feelings of gratitude that will keep you in an abundance mindset.

+ + + MINDSET CHECK-IN + + +

What's coming up for you? Write down all your fears about your goals. Are you afraid of failing? Are you thinking of problems that might occur if you succeed? Question each thought. Label your thought distortions.

Mind reading = MR | Fortune-telling = FT
All-or-nothing thinking = AON

Notice which thoughts aren't serving you.

Step Two: Start with the Big Picture

Writing down your goals is a great first step, but without taking inspired action, goal setting is merely magical thinking. Goal setting is important because it casts the vision for where you want to go and helps you with goal *getting*. Goals are destinations, and you need a plan or a road map to get there. The way I like to think about achieving my goals is to back into them. This means that when I do a planning session, I plug into my calendar promotion dates for shows, online class launches, and other important deadlines. Then I back out of the goal to see which tasks I'll need to plan for. For example, if I'm hosting an in-person event on May 1, I'll want to send out invitations three weeks prior. That mailing date goes on the calendar. Then I plug in my deadline for when the postcards must be ordered from the printer so that I can address them on time. Working backward from your goals will help you identify these deadlines. I repeat this process throughout the year, creating a list of tasks that must get done that help me get to my destination.

Take the goals you created in step one and plug in all your promotion dates and deadlines for creating your products. For goals that require you to do something, such as creating content or art, define both your due dates and your "do" dates. In other words, specify when you plan to create and when you plan to finish. In the example above, I would plan for the date to do the postcard design, the date to order them, the date to address them, and the date to mail them. Create this macro-plan from a bird's-eye view. For example, "In March, I'll create a five-piece collection" rather than deciding on "Monday at two." That type of micro-planning comes later.

Step Three: Break Your Goal into Milestones

Failure to break each goal into manageable pieces is a common stumbling block in achieving goals. For example, a promotion goal to launch an online class is too overwhelming to swallow whole, and just thinking about it might cause you angst. Break such a goal into small chunks: creating content for the online class, prospecting for students, creating promotional pieces, and any other necessary steps. Then, a large goal like that becomes much more manageable.

Here's an example you can try. I challenge you to add one hundred new email subscribers to your list this month. If you're worried this is too many, know it's only five new people each weekday. You can also move more slowly toward the same destination with a smaller goal, such as twenty new subscribers per month. Committing to even a turtle plan still yields big results. Generating twenty new subscribers each month will add 240 new subscribers in a year. The key is your commitment.

Identify all the steps you can take toward achieving each milestone. For example, to add five new subscribers to your email list per day, you may need to ask ten people, or perhaps create a promotional piece that you'll be able to get in front of one hundred people. Once you break down a goal this way, it will feel more achievable. Then you can go to work executing your plan. Repeat this process with all of your goals.

Set task-based goals. The secret to goal getting (rather than just goal setting) is to set weekly task-based goals, rather than outcome-based goals. Your goals for the year may be based on an outcome, such as your number of sales. However, a task-based goal is something over which you have complete control and which will move you closer to your desired outcome. Keep in mind that while a given task may not always get you to that outcome, at least you control whether you complete the task. For example, if your goal is to sell a certain amount of art via email on Black Friday, you can't control the number of people who will buy your art (the outcome), but you have complete control over writing the necessary promotional emails and scheduling them to go out. If your goal is building your email list, the number of subscribers you add to your list is the outcome; asking a certain number of people to join your email list each day is your task. And completing the task of asking a specific number of people each day is a goal over which you have total control.

Identify your priorities for the week. Each week, tackle three task-based goals that will get you closer to the outcomes you want to achieve. Enter all three in your planner. I use a planner with a full-week view so I can see all my appointments, tasks, and goals for the week at a glance. I always keep this full-size planner open on my desk. Use whatever works best for you. Writing down these tasks will keep them top of mind and keep you focused on what you want to accomplish each week. Each day, decide on the tasks you need to complete to make progress on your task-based outcomes for the week. For example, if one of my goals is to record a new podcast for the week, I know I'll have smaller steps to take to complete it. All the steps get added to my planner.

It's critical that the milestones you set for yourself each week are ones whose tasks you can accomplish during that time frame. For example, if you were building a website, that would be a huge undertaking, and not appropriate for a task-based goal to be achieved in one week. Rather, it's a goal that's perfect for breaking into more manageable chunks. A better weekly goal might be creating the "About" page for your website, or an even smaller goal, such as drafting the copy for that page. In breaking your large goal into these smaller bites, you'll make it less likely that you'll choke on it!

Share your goals. Sharing your weekly goals with others creates external accountability and helps reaffirm your commitment. Dr. Gail Matthews's research backs this up. In her Dominican University study, research participants who sent weekly progress reports to their friends accomplished significantly more than those who didn't. Dr. Matthews concluded that the role of public commitment added an additional layer of support. Her study provides proof of the effectiveness of three key tools toward achieving goals: accountability, commitment, and writing down your goals.[4]

Create a schedule. Creating your schedule begins with mapping out your ideal week. In my college's Academic Skills Center, they printed for us stacks of blank weekly schedules. At the beginning of each semester, I grabbed a stack of them and mapped out my ideal week, blocking time for exercise, meals with friends, classes, and study blocks, which I color-coded with neon highlighters. I didn't schedule every minute of the day, but by blocking time to study, I released the guilt that had come from imagining that I should always be working. I created space to enjoy free time. That freshman fall semester, I scraped by with a C+ in the physics course, but by senior year I had become a ninja at managing my time and study habits, which improved my grades without requiring me to sacrifice sleep.

Block your time. With time blocking, you can manage both your time and your priorities. When I create my ideal schedule now, I use theme days or theme time blocks, and I encourage you to do the same. For example, for me, Mondays and Fridays are "Zoom free"; I don't normally allow people to schedule calls or podcast interviews with me on those days. In addition, I keep my mornings free of appointments so I can have "genius time" for creative work that requires a lot of decisions. I want to give my best self to my creativity.

If you have young children at home, you may need to schedule your time differently. When that was my situation, my mornings were for computer time, and the afternoons, until three o'clock, were for creative time. Doing the admin work in the morning helped me clear brain clutter for the rest of the day; however, that was back when there was a lot less admin work to do! Now I make sure that my mornings are dedicated to "genius time" for creating art or writing. This is because throughout the day you'll be confronted with decisions, and as we discussed in chapter 4, decision-making is hard. The more decisions you make throughout the day, the less ability you'll have to make decisions well, which is known as decision fatigue.[5] You want to use your best decision-making power for creative decisions, not mundane ones like admin work. As the number of administrative tasks increased, I hired admin help in my business so I could focus on my children after three o'clock. I called the business help I hired the "business babysitter."

People find different ways to balance parenthood, marketing, and creativity. For example, my client Faye, who had custody of her children every other week, created theme weeks. She dedicated herself to artmaking during the time her ex-husband spent with the children, and she worked on administrative tasks during the weeks when her children were home. On the other hand, stay-at-home dad and full-time artist Patrick Guindon wakes up at five o'clock each morning to carve out time for art. Being intentional with your days enables you to create a weekly schedule that works for you.

Plan each week. At the start of the week, either Sunday night or first thing on Monday, I sit down with a physical planner in one hand and a digital calendar in the other to block out my time. Why both? The digital calendar allows me to schedule reminders on my phone and computer, and to use a host of scheduling tools with my friends, clients, and team. The paper planner lets me process the information in a different way, and, frankly, it makes planning more fun. I decorate my paper planner with color-coordinated washi tape and stickers. For those who haven't yet discovered the joy of washi tape, it's a decorative adhesive tape made from traditional Japanese paper (*wa* meaning "Japanese" and *shi* meaning "paper") that's great for crafting or journaling. The other advantage of the paper calendar is that I can keep it open on my desk to keep my priorities, goals, and tasks front of mind—and if I think of something I need to get done, I can just write it down before I forget it.

When you sit down with your calendar to do your weekly scheduling, first enter all of your appointments; then schedule all of your self-care and personal time, such as exercise or family events (and time for yourself to eat!). Then, identify your "big three" goal-oriented tasks for the week. With those tasks in mind, map out what other tasks need to be handled during those work blocks.

Never schedule out a vague work block, like "work" or "create." Assign a specific result that you'll need for every work block. For example, a work block could be "edit photos of new artwork." Describe what you plan to accomplish during each work block, and when you look at your schedule, you'll see your results in advance. By deciding ahead of time exactly what will be done during the work block, you'll reduce decision fatigue and minimize the risk that you'll start spinning—or worse, procrasti-learning. Establishing the work to get done during those work blocks forces you to prioritize.

When you time block, don't plan out every minute. Keep some white space around your work blocks and build in buffers and overflow time so you can catch up at the end of the week in case something unexpected comes up and derails your efforts. But to limit the chances of that happening, set firm work-hour boundaries. I always get more done when I limit my work hours because it forces me to focus on what's most important, rather than what feels urgent. Creativity loves constraints, and I find that I'm always more creative when I set time boundaries around my creative time. Many reality television shows, such as *Project Runway*, force contestants to complete a creative challenge within a given time frame. The contestants that make it until the end learn how to manage design projects that can be done within the time limits. In addition, although some experts advocate creating daily, I'm not one of them. I find that I work better when I take the weekends off to refill my creative well, so I don't do *any* work, including creative work, on the weekends.

Batch content. The hardest part of creating is getting started. It's challenging to start a project from scratch, and it's also hard to return to a project after a break. That's why it's helpful to batch similar tasks. Batching comes from the world of baking. When you make cupcakes, it wouldn't make sense to mix the ingredients to make a single cupcake, wait for it to bake, and then frost that single cupcake. Yet we do this all the time in our lives with our tasks.

By doing the same kind of work until it's done, you keep your momentum going because you stay in the mood to do that kind of work. For example, I'll group together all my photos that need to be edited for a single editing session. When you batch similar tasks together, you never have time to feel detached from the process, and, most importantly, you don't waste time getting into creating mode.

Research has shown that batching makes you more effective because it reduces multitasking. The *New Yorker* reported that 98 percent of people focus best when facing a single type of task, instead of multiple tasks.[6] For me, the most time-consuming task—and one that pulls me away from my creativity—is writing marketing emails and content for social media, and many artists I coach have the same issue. To limit this distraction from creativity, in one marathon session I write all my social media content for the month. This usually takes up an entire afternoon. I also take a few hours to compose my marketing emails for the month. (In general, a weekly email to connect with your audience is ideal, and then plan for additional emails when you're promoting something special.) By batching my most time-consuming tasks, for the rest of the month my brain is free to focus on creativity, which of course is what I enjoy most. But marketing content builds your audience and helps them connect to you, so whether you like it or not, batch it and get it over and done with.

I invest in tools that allow me to schedule those emails and social media posts throughout the month. The small monthly investment for these tools buys me so much freedom. And since I have an assistant, I give her the social media copy I've written and tell her which images I want her to schedule with each caption on social media. I delegate the scheduling because that's a task that doesn't need to be done by me. She does all the scheduling in one big batch session once a month. If we stopped to schedule each post as I wrote them, it would take substantially longer. Even if you don't have an assistant, you'll be more productive if you separate those tasks into the two buckets of creating and scheduling.

As you work, don't shift between unrelated tasks. John Medina wrote in his book *Brain Rules* that switching between various tasks can make projects take up to 50 percent longer to complete.[7] It's best to decide which kinds of like tasks you can group together, and then focus on a single batch of similar tasks. For example, when you complete a collection, photograph all your art in one batch. Then list all your products on the website in a different batch. If you photograph each artwork as you create it and then stop to list each on your website, it will slow you down.

Incorporate exercise into your schedule. I find incorporating regular exercise into my daily routine important not just for my waistline but also for my creativity and focus—because vigorous exercise gets the mind into a rhythm of creating. A 2014 Stanford study found that exercising on a regular basis, especially walking or some other type of aerobic exercise, can help foster creativity.[8] I block time for exercise at approximately the same time each day. I no longer choose the "best" instructor or the "best" class; I choose the one that fits my morning schedule so I can get on with my day. Exercising your body helps you compensate for spending long hours doing sedentary work, such as creating art or writing content. Although exercise takes time, it's worth having the sharper mind you get when your body has burned off all its nervous energy. After all, that's why Brahmin priests developed yoga over five thousand years ago—to prepare the mind and body for greater consciousness.[9]

Step Four: Track Your Progress

Track your progress, because if you don't, you won't be able to associate your actions with results, and you won't know what's working and what isn't. For example, things you've done for a long time may not be as effective as they used to be—so you'll want to check regularly to see whether what you're doing is working, so you can pivot when it isn't. Let's say you wanted to lose weight and you ordered one of those brand-name meal-delivery services, but soon found that you were gaining weight instead of losing it; you'd change your plan, right? The same thing is true with your creative business. Keep an eye on how things are working—especially your new efforts—and decide whether you need to tweak something or do something completely different.

When I helped my client Tracy grow her email list, I suggested she note how many subscribers she started with and see how much her list grew each day. She added fifty names in twenty-four hours, and in two weeks she had added more than five hundred names to her list. Tracking her progress added fuel to her fire. Watching her email list grow motivated Tracy to lean into our strategy even harder, producing greater results.

There are many ways to track your progress. You can use a spreadsheet, or create a place in a physical planner for keeping track. For reading goals, I've kept a list in the back of my planner of books I've finished. Other times I've posted a goal chart on my studio wall, which keeps them top of mind. Some people like to give themselves gold stars or stickers. Delight yourself so the tracking is more fun than a chore.

Step Five: Celebrate Your Wins

Celebrating progress is key to achieving any goal. But if you're feeling stuck or disappointed with your progress, you're not alone; we've all been there when things don't go the way we hope and expect. Try not to focus on all the things going wrong, though, as that's exhausting and demotivating. Keep your focus on what's going right, and it will elevate both your mood and your motivation.

Humans evolved to focus on problems as a survival mechanism. (Remember: we evolved for survival, not goal achievement.) If we're not intentional, we can let the negative outweigh the wins and the good moments. As Dr. Valerie Rein, author of *Patriarchy Stress Disorder*, said, "Our brain is conditioned to track threat. That's just a survival adaptation, survival of the anxious. . . . Because that is such strong wiring, we have a tendency of bypassing things that are going well and that are giving us joy and pleasure. And so, it takes a conscious effort to rewire that and train our attention and our whole system to register and imprint positive experiences."[10]

Rein calls this process taking the time to "imprint the wins." To counteract our negativity bias, she says you need to take ten seconds for mindful focus on your positive experiences in order to internalize them. Research by Rick Hanson and Rick Mendius supports this claim, and they say the brain is "hard-wired to scan for the bad, and when it inevitably finds negative things, they're both stored immediately plus made available for rapid recall. In contrast, positive experiences (short of million-dollar moments) are usually registered through standard memory systems, and thus need to be held in conscious awareness ten to twenty seconds for them to really sink in."[11] Rein also elaborated that taking time throughout the day to enjoy mundane pleasures, from a cup of coffee to beautiful weather, will retrain your brain to grow your pleasure-receiving muscle.

When you celebrate your progress, measure against your starting point. Focus on how far you've come, not how far you have to go. When you track your progress in a way that shows what you've already achieved, you'll stay motivated. If you're always looking at how far you have to go, you may feel as though you're failing, which will make it more likely that you'll give up.

Practice counting wins. My husband uses his short drive home from the office to do a mental accounting of his daily wins. When my children were younger, we did this as a family around the dinner table. We didn't call it counting wins; instead, we simply talked about the best part of the day or the week. This moved the conversation from one of complaining to a better outlook. The point of this practice isn't to ignore negative and painful emotions. Of course, it's important to process negative emotions, too, but as we have a natural tendency to pay attention to the negative already, counting wins gives you a process for redirecting your focus.

Count all inspired actions taken, and not just desired outcomes, as wins. For example, writing an email to your list is an inspired action that should be celebrated. Inspired actions often lead to inspired outcomes, but it's better to be detached from the outcome. If you worry about the likelihood of making a sale every time you write another email, you'll have more anxiety about writing it.

Write down your wins. Acknowledging your wins is great, but it's still easy to forget the goodness that has come into your life. Inside my planner, I maintain a column for keeping track of my wins for the week. When I write down a win, I've noticed that I've been way more likely to take another positive action sooner. Write down your wins in a place where you can see them accumulating throughout the week. Other artists I know incorporate positive thinking as part of their morning pages, nightly journaling, or gratitude practice. There isn't a right or wrong way to do this, but keeping track of wins in a place that's visible helps keep your mindset positive.

Vocalize your wins. When you share your wins with a partner, friend, family member, or peer group, and they respond positively, your positive feelings last longer. That's why joining a professional peer group, such as a mastermind, is so powerful. When other people cheer you on, it enhances your happy feelings and amplifies your success. I ask my mastermind members to share their wins for the week before discussing challenges. Members also feel motivated by hearing other people's wins and are more likely to tackle a new strategy when they witness their peers succeed in doing it.

When you're sharing wins, people love the positivity. They feel your positive energy, they want to be around you, and that makes your environment, at home or at work, a happier place. On the other hand, complaining is the opposite of sharing wins. No one wants to be around a complaining Eeyore. Some people wear complaining as a badge of honor. But unless you're a comedian who has mastered the art of humorous complaining, your complaining won't be funny; it will instead suck the joy out of the room.

If you believe that there's not enough abundance to go around, you may feel unhappy when someone else celebrates their wins. If this happens to you, learn to check the feeling and recognize that other people's success is proof of what's possible for you. This will help loosen any resistance you have to the success you're seeking. And the more you practice allowing abundance instead of resisting it, the easier you'll find it. Through belief, we replace doubt with abundance.

Many of the artists I coach start believing in the possibility for their own success when they see others in the program succeeding. For example, wildlife artist Elizabeth Mordensky surpassed her income goal even while working a full-time job. She shared that gaining inspiration from the other students played a huge role in her success. She noticed that the artists who were getting opportunities were asking for them. "And so that's what I did. I've heard lots of nos, but the yeses have been big. I'll take the yeses." By taking charge and reaching out, she went on to get a feature article in *Western Art Collector* magazine, which resulted in $9,500 in art sales.[12]

Focus on what's already working. Though we tend to focus on the obstacles before us, giving attention to problems prolongs them. When we feel negative, it takes us longer to get our work done and create. Plus, if you list everything that's going wrong, notice what happens in your body. Is your jaw clenching? Are you grinding your teeth? Are your shoulders hunching? When I used to watch the news, I could feel my stomach turn with the panic porn that daily news media dishes out. Now that I limit my news media (and social media), I feel lighter.

You may be tempted to focus on what you need to improve or change, but there's an advantage to doubling down on what's already working for you. Instead of chasing a new strategy or social media platform, ask yourself, "How can I lean into this?" Look at all the ways you've already sold your art, what kind of art it was, and how you sold it. Lean into that. Ask yourself, "Why is it working so well?" You might be tempted to analyze who unsubscribes, but it's always a mistake to focus on the people who don't want what you've got. Success comes when you focus on the people who love you and when you love them up even more.

Another advantage of focusing on what's working is that you'll boost your self-esteem. If you think only about your setbacks or failures, of course you're going to feel lousy. On the other hand, when you focus on the steps you're taking toward your goals, you'll feel like you're winning at something. So many times we feel like we need somebody to help us out of a funk or to encourage us, when in reality we've had that power all along.

If you're having a bad day or feeling discouraged, pause to identify at least three things that went well during the day, even if the day ended poorly. What tasks did you get done? What did you accomplish? Remember that all inspired actions, and not just desired outcomes, are steps in the right direction. Keeping your focus on what's working will help you maintain a better state of mind and build momentum.

Step Six: Enlist Help

Often, we reach a point where a DIY effort causes more harm than good. Just because you *can* do something doesn't mean you *should*—and sometimes you'll even save money by hiring someone else to do a task, because they can do it faster or better while you're left free to work in your zone of genius. For example, when I discovered that a significant portion of the emails I sent to my list of subscribers was going to their spam folders, I paid a freelancer thirty-five dollars to fix this for me. I didn't have to learn the difference between SPF, DKIM, and DMARC; I just paid someone who knew what to do. Our time and energy are limited. We can always make more money, but we can't make more time than the twenty-four hours we're given.

Outsource anything that can be done faster, cheaper, or better by someone else. When my husband and I were first married, he used to iron all his own shirts. Once the babies came and life got busy, we began sending the shirts out with the rest of the dry cleaning, which saved him at least an hour each week. When I discovered a dry cleaner with delivery service, I stopped dropping off and picking up every week, which saved me the hassle of packing cranky little ones into a car for an unnecessary errand. That's why I was a bit surprised when my husband suggested he start ironing his own shirts again to save money.

"You're kidding me. What would we save, like ten dollars a week?" I tried to soften my voice, because I know my husband hates when I get know-it-all-y on him. "Sweetie, how much do you charge per hour? I mean, does it make sense for you to be spending your time ironing shirts when you can outsource that for a lot less than you're making in one billable hour?" My husband was focusing on getting the ironing done cheaper, without considering the impact that doing it himself would have on his ability to make money.

In our businesses, we often think we'll save money when we do a job ourselves, but if that task can be done better, faster, or cheaper by someone else (and at least two of these requirements can be fulfilled), don't hesitate to outsource it. Business coach Jen Lehner, who helps small business owners create systems for their businesses, told me, "The first thing you need to get off your plate is the thing that you hate the most, that you just really can't stand, that you do repetitively. . . . For some people that's managing their inbox or invoicing or chasing down clients for contracts to get signed."[13] For many people, housework will be the first task that gets outsourced (like my husband's ironing).

In the early days of my business, I had high school interns help me with social media, listing my art on Etsy or my website, packing and shipping prints, and other tasks. I paid these "business babysitters" the going rate for literal babysitters in my area, which was a great trade-off for me. Instead of doing everything myself and hiring help to watch my kids, I had help with all the tasks that didn't need to be done by me so I could spend more time with my children.

Now that I've been in business for over twenty years, I enlist professional help all the time. For example, I have someone who edits my podcast, and a team member who creates the graphics for social media. I still cast the vision, write my own podcast episodes, and art-direct the look, but I don't execute everything myself. Whenever I find myself doing a non-art task, I pause to ask, "Does this have to be done by me?" I also ask, "Does this have to be done at all?" and "Does this have to be done by a human?" Always eliminate nonessential tasks and automate as much as possible. If you can't eliminate or automate a menial task, you can give it to an assistant.

Having someone on your side can make a huge difference when you feel alone in your business. With people helping you, you don't have to feel like everything is up to you and you can talk to someone other than your cat (or maybe that's just me).

Invest in a coach. There are times when I can't see the path forward in my business. That's when I enlist help in the form of a mentor or a coach. I've invested tens of thousands of dollars over the years in coaching and masterminds, but I've almost always found the help I get is worth it. This is because it helps me avoid mistakes, which saves me time and money.

If you wanted to go for a walk along the beach or around your neighborhood, you wouldn't need a guide, right? If you wanted to go hiking, you might need help. If you wanted to go rock climbing, you'd be a fool to go alone. Making it as an artpreneur can be like rock climbing, with unpredictable ups and downs. Having a coach is a great advantage toward building a successful business—especially if you want to enjoy the experience.

Todd Herman, peak performance coach and author of *The Alter Ego Effect*, shared this with me: "The biggest mistake that I made early on in life was I had that ego where I wanted to climb to the top of the mountain on my own and plant that flag up there and say, 'I did it and I did it all on my own. I didn't get any help to get up here.' It wasn't until I met a mentor, and he just sort of laughed at me, as that's one of the stupidest and slowest ways you could ever reach success."[14] Now, you might be thinking, "I've got this and can do it on my own." If that's you, I applaud you. However, what often stands in the way of the struggling artists are emotional triggers such as doubt and fear about what you need to do. If you aren't sure what to do next, you'll probably end up doing nothing, or worse, spend your time spinning doing the wrong things. But it could be that you lack the strategy knowledge to build a solid foundation. You can learn this the hard way with years of trial and error, wasting time, money, and opportunities, or you can follow a formula that's been proven over and over again so you never have to second-guess or doubt your next move. The key to success in any business starts with knowing what you know and seeking out expert guidance for what you don't. If you imagine that the best Olympic athletes in the world all have coaches, why shouldn't we?

Step Seven: Master the Emotional Side of Productivity

If I could program your brain, like Keanu Reeves in *The Matrix*, you would be all set, but as humans, we've got emotions that get in the way. Here's how to master the emotional side of productivity.

Choose a word or a theme. When I'm doing my annual brainstorming and setting my vision and goals for the year, I always find it helpful to choose a theme or a word. I choose a word that describes how I want to feel or who I want to become. Some words that I've chosen include "evolve," "harmony," "inspire," and "purpose." I use the word as a rallying point when I create my goals. The word gives me a motivational push to start the year, but as the year progresses, I also find it helpful to choose a word for the day. When I sit at my desk to see what I need to do during the day, I'll choose one word to describe the kind of person I want to be that day, and I'll journal about why I chose it.

Imagine opening a closet with all the feelings you could put on and picking the emotion that will fuel you. When you need a productive day, choose a word like "determined." When you have a day that will require courage, choose a word such as "confidence." You can choose how you want to feel—and this helps.

Meditate. I've noticed both long-term and short-term benefits from meditating. Research published in *JAMA* in 2014 also concluded that "mindfulness meditation programs had moderate evidence of improved anxiety."[15] When I meditate in the morning, I'm calm and focused the rest of the day, and it's easier for me to concentrate during long stretches of working in the studio. Meditation has also helped me let go of negative thought patterns. This helps me quiet my inner critic while I'm painting or writing.

Quiet the inner critic. You cannot do your best work if you're constantly critiquing yourself. (This is why the creative process and the editing process must be separated.) If I work in silence, or even to music, critical voices start chiming in with their opinions whether I want them to or not. Sometimes the voices aren't even criticizing my art, but simply reminding me of unpleasant thoughts. In either case, the voices are unhelpful distractions. (And my inner critic always speaks in a mean, sarcastic tone.) Although meditation has helped with this tremendously, I've found that the best way for me to quiet my inner critic while working on visual art is to listen to a podcast or audiobook. I prefer narratives over music because the voice in my head gets drowned out by a different voice.

You might imagine that silence helps you focus more intently, but the muse often works best when your conscious mind is distracted, and your subconscious mind takes over. For many creative types, especially those with ADHD, research has shown that background noise or white noise improves both concentration and abstract thinking.[16] For tasks that require writing, instrumental music is helpful in overcoming the inner critic.

Stop ruminating. Sometimes you'll be distracted by your own thoughts even when you're using the methods described here. If you're distracted by thoughts of something else you need to do, instead of switching tasks, enter that new task in your planner. Often, when we can't stop ruminating, just writing down the thought provides relief. David Allen, author of *Getting Things Done*, says, "Everything you've told yourself you ought to do, your mind thinks you should do right now."[17] Therefore, he recommends writing down everything that needs to be done to alleviate stress. It assures your brain that you don't need to be reminded. I like to think of writing down tasks the way Dumbledore siphoned off memories to put them in a Pensieve. When you write down your thoughts, imagine pulling the silvery thread from your mind and depositing it in your journal.

WHAT ARTPRENEURS NEED TO BELIEVE

- Each time you do what you say you're going to do, you bolster your self-trust.
- You're not going to go any further than your dream (so dream *big*!).
- Learning how to set goals and then manage your priorities will enable you to focus your valuable time on the five foundations of the Passion-to-Profit framework.
- All inspired actions taken, not just desired outcomes, count as wins.

MARCHING ORDERS

- Write down your goals.
- Start with the big picture.
- Break your goals into milestones.
- Track your progress.
- Celebrate your wins along the way.
- Enlist help.
- Use a word as a rallying point for a motivational push.
- Meditate to quiet your mind.

"THERE ARE MOMENTS
WHEN YOU DON'T SELL
ANYTHING . . . THE PHONE
ISN'T RINGING, YOU'RE NOT
INSPIRED, AND I THINK
THAT'S WHERE WE REALLY
FIND OUT WHO WE ARE . . .
THOSE MOMENTS IN
BETWEEN ALL THE ACTION."

—ASHLEY LONGSHORE[1]

KEEP MARCHING
FORWARD

THE SCHOOL BUS BUMPED ALONG past the yellow-and-orange
fall foliage. Checking my reflection in the window, I reached
up to scrunch up my eighties Jersey-style curls. In the middle of
ninth grade, following my mother's separation from her second
husband, we moved in with my grandparents in New Jersey. It
was the sixth time I had to change schools. By the time I reached
high school, I'd found that the easiest way to make friends was
to sign up for extracurriculars, like drama and debate team, because the artsy drama kids were always more accepting of my
quirkiness. However, by senior year I was overscheduled. Worse,
I had a full-blown case of senioritis and regretted the promise I'd
made the previous spring to serve as speech and debate president. Most of my debate-team friends had graduated, and I
didn't feel like sitting on the bus next to the newbies. Instead, I
chose a seat just behind the bus driver, beside our beloved
drama teacher, Mr. Endalkatchew, a slim, well-dressed Black
man in his early thirties.

I first met Mr. E during sophomore year, when I painted the backdrops for the school play. The following year, I had a small role in the fall play and got to know him better. Often in the world of high school productions, your parts get better as you develop a relationship with the director and earn seniority; however, I missed out on the auditions completely in the spring because I overscheduled myself (more on that in a moment). Then, I hoped for a bigger part my senior year but was disappointed that he wasn't directing the school play at all. He also stepped down as the speech and debate coach. Instead, he only occasionally chaperoned our team to weekly tournaments.

Meanwhile, a mountain of assignments weighed down on me. Overloaded with the drama club, AP classes, and now this event, my hope of squeezing in some homework between tournament rounds was futile. Fantasizing about getting past the college admissions process (and the relief I anticipated coming with it), I sighed. "I can't wait until the spring when I'm done with all this."

Mr. E turned his head sharply to look at me and hissed, "Don't ever wish to rush time." His words hit me like a slap in the face.

When Mr. E chastised me, I thought it was due to his obsession with existentialism, which suggests that every individual is responsible for creating meaning or purpose in their lives. I had been introduced to the philosophy during junior year when I prepped for an audition for No Exit by Jean-Paul Sartre. Mr. E had chosen the 1944 existentialist's work for the spring performance. The play tells the story of three departed souls trapped in a room together. Embroiled in an unrequited love triangle, their personal hell turns out to be each other. I imagined myself starring as one of the femme fatales, and on the morning of the audition, I carefully lined my eyes in the style of a 1940s pinup girl and borrowed my mother's silk fuchsia blouse to wear to school.

Although the audition was scheduled for the same afternoon as my weekly piano lesson, I thought I could squeeze in both. Unfortunately, the piano teacher ran late with the student before me, and my lesson went into overtime as well (partly because I'd been practicing lines from the play, not my piano music). In vain, I sprinted the full mile between my teacher's garlic-scented home back to the high school. By the time I arrived, smelling faintly of garlic, sweat stains blooming under each armpit, and eyeliner streaking down my face, I no longer looked the part of a French seductress. Moreover, the drama club room was completely empty, except for Mr. E.

"Well, I guess I won't have to explain to you why you didn't get cast," he joked. Succumbing to the pointlessness of trying to squeeze everything in, I burst into tears. Looking at me thoughtfully, he asked, "What happened?"

Blowing my nose into a tissue, I didn't blame my piano teacher. I knew I'd spread myself too thin among extracurriculars I didn't care about. I may not have been destined for the stage (or Carnegie Hall for that matter), but racing back and forth and chasing too many activities wasn't the answer. I quit piano later that month. However, if I had fully learned my lesson when I missed out on the *No Exit* audition, I probably wouldn't have been sitting on that bus.

A few months after our conversation on the school bus, I sat in the high school auditorium waiting for the curtain to rise on a different existentialist play, Samuel Beckett's *Waiting for Godot*. Instead of running a student production, Mr. E staged a "passion project" performance with two other English teachers. His slight frame made him perfectly suited to play the frail Estragon. During the emotionally charged climax that ended the play, Endalkatchew's Estragon dropped to his knees and cried out in anguish, "I can't go on like this!" to which his companion replied, "That's what you think."

The plot of this play centers around the hopelessness of the two main characters in an endless quest to meet Godot, who never arrives. They while away the day, further underlining the pointlessness of their own lives as they wait for something better.

But that something better, that perfect time, never arrives. At its core, existentialism maintains that individuals must create value by affirming it and living it, not simply by talking about it or dreaming about it. When the play ends, we as an audience feel a sense of relief, leaving behind the inertia of the two characters stuck in their bleak wasteland, while we're free to move forward with our lives.

In the end, the life lesson for me came not from the play or the school bus. A year after I graduated, news reached me at college that Jasper Endalkatchew had lost his life in the worsening AIDS pandemic. His words, "Don't ever wish to rush time," finally made sense.

If you're nursing the dream of becoming an artpreneur, take inspired action now. Don't just dream or talk about when you'll find time. Wishing for the perfect future that may never happen isn't the answer.

Choosing what's most essential is a lesson I need to remind myself of repeatedly. Even in high school, I couldn't take piano lessons *and* try out for the play. I had to ask myself which was more important to me, and why. If your art is most important, you won't have time to waste on random acts of marketing. That's why I boiled down the essentials of selling your art to five time-less marketing foundations that will work no matter what social media platform comes along next. Sadly, I see so many artists racing back and forth between platforms and commitments. And when you're spread thin, you're racing toward mediocrity. But when you do what matters most and eliminate what doesn't work, you'll have more time for your creativity.

WHY YOUR ART MATTERS

We've talked about how to make your way in this world as an artpreneur, and how to tap into the psychology of buyers and build a stronger mindset in order to sell more art. But remember that your art matters in so many ways beyond what selling it will do for you professionally. Art helps us process the world around us, and serves both a spiritual and social function, not unlike religion. The Beckett play may have helped a young man come to terms with his AIDS diagnosis, and a fatherless teenage girl in the audience understand the importance of the here and now. Life continues to show us how short and precious it is.

As a teenager on that bus, I thought my life began after exams. As an analyst on Wall Street, I waited for the big bonus each year, but after 9/11 I knew my dreams could no longer wait. Perhaps you, too, are hearing whispers from the universe. In the Great Resignation of 2021, over four million people walked away from their jobs.[2] There's nothing like a crisis to lift the veil on what's no longer working for you—whether that's a commute you hate, an abusive boss, or simply a position that's not aligned with your values.

Whether it's words for the stage, paint on the canvas, or music for the soul, art gives our lives meaning. Artists show the world, through their poems, pictures, notes, and dance, that there's hope. Some of the most beloved art has risen from the ashes of world wars, nuclear bombs, genocide, and other tragedies. As an artist, you're part of the healing that the world needs—from both its personal and collective traumas. In *Waiting for Godot*, Beckett suggests that religion is an illusion that gives humans hope and meaning. Your *art* gives the world hope and meaning.

But art only helps people when they know about it. And that's why I've written this book for you. When you work on your production plan, you'll create art in your own authentic voice. When you market your art, you get feedback on what kind of art resonates with your audience. When you price your art appropriately, you'll teach the world that your art is valuable, and the world will stand up and take notice. When you prospect to build an audience, you connect with those who need your art.

Promote your art to reach more people with your message—not only to sell it, but because your art matters.

DON'T BLAME YOUR BOOTS

When you're doing everything you're supposed to, but not enjoying immediate success, you may wonder, "Is all this worth it?" Unfortunately, many people give up too soon. Remember, at first, your business is a baby. It demands a lot of attention and can't stand up on its own. As your business grows, the adolescent years aren't much easier. You won't have full control of every circumstance or even the speed of results from the actions you take—but you'll have full control of whether you continue to take those actions. The artists who finally make it as artpreneurs are the ones who don't blame their boots for poor results.[3] They continue putting one foot in front of the other, making forward progress and marching ahead (not running in place!). Keep taking inspired action, and positive results will follow.

ACKNOWLEDGMENTS

+ + + + + + + +

I'm someone who always skips to the back of the book to read the acknowledgments, and if that's you, too, I see you!

I stand on the shoulders of a lot of very smart people. Thank you to Linda Sivertsen and Allison Lane for helping me shape the proposal from a cringey memoir to prescriptive how-to. Thank you to Michele Martin for taking it over the finish line and for all the times you helped me navigate the traditional book publishing world. Thank you to Candice L. Davis for your insightful edits, friendship, and cheerleading. Much gratitude to my publicist Barbara Teszler, who rode in on her white horse and unlocked press opportunities I'd never dreamed of while staying aligned with our values.

Huge thank-you to Sara Kendrick for taking the chance on a first-time author shaking up HarperCollins with a quirky Jewish New Yorker. On the HarperCollins team, I had not one but three badass women all making sure I didn't stick my foot in my mouth. Thank you to Linda Alila for adding "hot girl" energy and her extensive knowledge of anthropology and inclusive lingerie brands; Ron Huizinga for matching my artist demands with an outstanding book cover; Heather Howell for handling all the back-end wizardry; Sicily Axton, Briá Woods, and Josh deLacy for marketing the shit out of it; Jeff Farr, Beth Metrick, Noah Perkins, and Aubrey Khan for making the layout look fantastic AF; Natalie Jones for keeping all the grammar kosher; Ellen Kadin for her tough love New Yorker brand of developmental edits; and the entire HCL team, some of whom I've never met but who all worked hard to bring this project together.

Thank you to the entire Inspiration Place team, who kept the business humming without a hiccup during the book-writing process. An especially huge thank-you goes to Anna Kuhlmey—I couldn't imagine running this business without you—as well as to Shaun Roney creating mental clarity for all our artist clients.

Thank you to all my friends and business besties, many of whom you met on these pages, as well as all the artists from The Artist Incubator who have allowed me to share their stories. It's been an honor helping you grow your art businesses.

Most of all, thank you to my children, Talia and Seth, who need not do anything for my love. I'm grateful just because you're here with me in this world.

However, I do have to give Talia a special thank-you for editing the first four chapters (and that's why they're better than the rest of the book) as well as to my mother for telling me how much she loved it when the editing process got tough. But most of all, thank you to Ron, my husband—you are truly my rock and my best friend.

And a huge thank-you to you, the reader, for picking up this book and for investing in your future success. As a gift, I'd like to give you exclusive access to The Artist Profit Plan. In this complimentary multimedia training, you'll learn cutting-edge techniques for "what's working now" in the world of selling art. You can find this completely free gift at **schulmanart.com/bookbonus**.

NOTES

+ + + + + + + +

CHAPTER 1

1. "The Beliefs That Defeat You, Part 1," *Feeling Good* (podcast), episode 118, December 10, 2018, https://feelinggood.com/2018/12/10/118-self -defeating-beliefs-part-1/.
2. Edward Lovett, "Most Models Meet Criteria for Anorexia, Size 6 Is Plus Size: Magazine," ABC News, January 13, 2012, https://abcnews.go.com /blogs/headlines/2012/01/most-models-meet-criteria-for-anorexia -size-6-is-plus-size-magazine/.
3. "Body Dysmorphia Among Male Teenagers and Men: What to Know," American Addiction Centers, updated February 25, 2022, https:// americanaddictioncenters.org/male-eating-disorders/body -dysmorphia.
4. A. Rochaun, "I Deserve to Take Up Space, and I Make No Apologies," Scary Mommy, August 17, 2019, https://www.scarymommy.com/black -woman-deserve-take-up-space/.
5. Joe Kindness, "Social Media Marketing vs. Email Marketing: Pros & Cons," Agency Analytics, February 17, 2021, https://agencyanalytics .com/blog/social-media-vs-email-marketing.
6. "Coffee with Marie Forleo: Chatting About Purpose, Time Stress & Eliminating a Workaholic Mentality," *Online Marketing Made Easy with Amy Porterfield* (podcast), episode #435, https://www.amyporterfield .com/435transcript/.
7. You can find *The Inspiration Place* podcast at https://www.schulmanart .com/podcast/ and the Artist Incubator Coaching Program at https:// www.schulmanart.com/biz/.

CHAPTER 2

1. Carol J. Loomis, "Warren Buffett's Wild Ride at Salomon," *Fortune*, October 27, 1997, https://fortune.com/1997/10/27warren-buffett -salomon/.

2. John Greenwald, "The California Wipeout," *Time*, December 19, 1994, https://content.time.com/time/subscriber/article/0,33009,982029,00 .html.

3. Floyd Norris, "Ex-Salomon Chief's Costly Battle," *New York Times*, August 19, 1994, https://www.nytimes.com/1994/08/19/business/ex -salomon-chief-s-costly-battle.html.

4. All client names have been changed to protect their privacy unless I've been given explicit permission to use their real names in this book.

5. "The World Trade Center Bombing: Report and Analysis," US Fire Administration, Technical Report Series USFA-TR-076, Washington, DC, February 1993, https://www.usfa.fema.gov/downloads/pdf /publications/tr-076.pdf.

6. Saul Hansell, "Salomon Will Start Selling Orange County Debt Today," *New York Times*, December 15, 1994, https://www.nytimes.com/1994/12 /15/business/salomon-will-start-selling-orange-county-debt-today .html.

7. Both Tim and Tom were Asian men. Although Asian Americans make up 15 percent of the workforce on Wall Street, rarely do they rise to C-suite positions, and as a result, they fill the ranks of middle management. (See Hugh Son, "Why Asian Americans on Wall Street from Goldman Sachs to Wells Fargo Are Breaking Their Silence," CNBC, May 21, 2021, https:// www.cnbc.com/2021/05/21/why-asian-americans-on-wall-street-are -breaking-their-silence.html.)

8. Because of the prestige and outrageous returns, *everyone* wanted to work for our hedge fund—including Tom. When he showed up for his interview, I knew exactly how to squash it. I cornered Tim and nodded in the direction of the conference room. With mock innocence, I asked, "I'm not sure why he's here. Do you think he wants *your* job?"

9. The "tie factor" has been documented in Roger Lowenstein's book *When Genius Failed: The Rise and Fall of Long-Term Capital Management* (Random House, 2001). Although the author invited me to contribute to his book, I was still employed by LTCM and so I declined to be interviewed. However, I remember joking about the correlation of ties to the severity of the situation.

10. "Caregiving in the United States 2020," AARP, May 14, 2020, https:// www.aarp.org/ppi/info-2020/caregiving-in-the-united-states.html; Nancy Kerr, "Family Caregivers Spend More Than $7,200 a Year on Out-of-Pocket Costs," AARP, June 29, 2021, https://www.aarp.org /caregiving/financial-legal/info-2021/high-out-of-pocket-costs.html.

11. "Number of Active Etsy Sellers from 2012 to 2019," statista.com, https:// www.statista.com/statistics/409374/etsy-active-sellers/.

12. "Etsy Number of Active Sellers, 2012–2021," Marketplace Pulse, https:// www.marketplacepulse.com/stats/etsy/etsy-number-of-active -sellers-2.

13. Charity L. Scott, "Etsy CEO Josh Silverman Stands by Strategy of Competing with Amazon," *Wall Street Journal*, April 12, 2022, https://www.wsj.com/articles/etsy-chief-executive-stands-by-strategy-of-competing-with-amazon-11649802297.

14. Jeffry Bartash, "U.S. Job Openings Hit Record 9.3 Million – But More People are Quitting Than Ever," MarketWatch, June 8, 2021, https://www.marketwatch.com/story/u-s-job-opening-leap-to-record-9-3-million-but-hiring-lags-well-behind-11623161366.

15. The title of Gabby Bernstein's book *The Universe Has Your Back: Transform Fear to Faith* (Hay House, 2016) is a beautiful mantra.

CHAPTER 3

1. Carlos De Loera, "The 'Hot Girl Summer' Meme, Explained," *Los Angeles Times*, July 19, 2019, https://www.latimes.com/entertainment-arts/music/story/2019-07-19/hot-girl-summer-meme-megan-thee-stallion-explained.

2. "Dr. Aaron T. Beck," Beck Institute, https://beckinstitute.org/about/dr-aaron-beck/.

3. Hara Estroff Marano, "Our Brain's Negativity Bias," *Psychology Today*, June 20, 2003, https://www.psychologytoday.com/us/articles/200306/our-brains-negative-bias.

4. Phoebe Hoban, *Alice Neel: The Art of Not Sitting Pretty* (David Zwirner Books, 2021), p. 12.

5. "Alice Neel," The Art Story, n.d., https://www.theartstory.org/artist/neel-alice/life-and-legacy/.

6. Zoe Goldman, "Yoko Ono, Betye Saar, Eva Hesse, Alice Neel, and Others Talk About Feminism, Motherhood, and Art," Getty, November 12, 2019, https://blogs.getty.edu/iris/yoko-ono-betye-saar-eva-hesse-alice-neel-feminism-motherhood-and-art/.

CHAPTER 4

1. Robert Browning, "Andrea del Sarto," Poetry Foundation, https://www.poetryfoundation.org/poems/43745/andrea-del-sarto.

2. When I shared this chapter with my daughter, she didn't believe me about the $455 T-shirts. After a second search on the Neiman Marcus site for "men's black T-shirt," sorted by price from high to low, we spotted a plain, logo-free Tom Ford long-sleeve black T-shirt for $1,690.

3. Chris Taylor, "Why Doesn't She Initiate?" Knowing Her Sexuality, January 9, 2020, https://khsministry.com/2020/01/09/why-doesnt-she-initiate/.

CHAPTER 5

1. Tom Hopkins and Laura Laaman, *The Certifiable Salesperson: The Ultimate Guide to Help Any Salesperson Go Crazy with Unprecedented Sales* (Wiley, 2002).
2. Juried shows are when visual artists will pay a fee to be judged for entry in a group show. In addition to being judged "worthy" of participation, the judges often award ribbons to the art they liked best.
3. "Take Up Space and Make Some Noise with Andrea Owen," *The Inspiration Place* (podcast), episode 160, September 28, 2021, https://www.schulmanart.com/transcript160/.
4. "Poverty Mindset with Erica Courdae," *The Inspiration Place* (podcast), episode 117, November 24, 2020, https://www.schulmanart.com/2020/11/117-poverty-mindset-with-erica-courdae/.
5. Trevor Wheelwright, "The Gender Pay Gap Across the US in 2022," Business.org, March 1, 2022, https://www.business.org/hr/benefits/gender-pay-gap/.
6. Sherri Kolade, "When Is It Their Turn? Black Women and the Ever-Widening Pay Gap," *New Pittsburgh Courier*, March 4, 2022, https://newpittsburghcourier.com/2022/03/04/when-is-it-their-turn-black-women-and-the-ever-widening-pay-gap/.
7. Jessica Testa, "Ella Emhoff Drops a Small (Very Small) Collection of Knits," *New York Times*, February 18, 2021, https://www.nytimes.com/2021/02/18/style/ella-emhoff-collection.html.
8. Dana Covit, "Gotta Have That Cute Mug? Act Fast," *New York Times*, May 10, 2021, https://www.nytimes.com/2021/05/10/style/ceramics-mug.html.
9. "Making Time for It All with Jeanne Oliver and Miriam Schulman," *The Inspiration Place* (podcast), episode 157, September 7, 2021, https://www.schulmanart.com/2021/09/157-making-time-for-it-all-with-jeanne-oliver-and-miriam-schulman/

CHAPTER 6

1. "How to Stand Out and Get Your Art Noticed with Jennifer Kem and Miriam Schulman," *The Inspiration Place* (podcast), episode 188, April 12, 2022, https://www.schulmanart.com/2022/04/188-how-to-stand-out-and-get-your-art-noticed-with-jennifer-kem-and-miriam-schulman/.
2. "Visibility + Vulnerability with India Jackson," *The Inspiration Place* (podcast), episode 110, October 6, 2020, https://www.schulmanart.com/2020/10/110-visibility-vulnerability-with-india-jackson/.
3. "Finding Your Signature Style in Art, Music, or Business with Jason Van Orden," *The Inspiration Place* (podcast), episode 0, August 20, 2018, https://www.schulmanart.com/2018/08/000-finding-your-signature-style-in-art-music-or-business-with-jason-van-orden/.

4. Camille Claudel was best known as both a sculptor and a muse. Art historians believe that Claudel carved the hands and feet of many of Rodin's sculptures during her apprenticeship in his studio.
5. Yayoi Kusama, Harry Shunk, János Kender, *The Anatomic Explosion*, 1968. MoMA / The Museum of Modern Art, https://www.moma.org/collection/works/177001.
6. "Your Heroic Character with Ron Reich," *The Inspiration Place* (podcast), episode 79, March 3, 2020, https://www.schulmanart.com/2020/03/079-your-heroic-character-with-ron-reich/.
7. "People Pleasing, Perfectionism & Procrastination with Shaun Roney," *The Inspiration Place* (podcast), episode 96, June 30, 2020, https://www.schulmanart.com/2020/06/096-people-pleasing-perfectionism-procrastination-with-shaun-roney/.
8. "The Hype Handbook with Michael F. Schein," *The Inspiration Place* (podcast), episode 133, March 23, 2021, https://www.schulmanart.com/2021/03/133-the-hype-handbook-with-michael-f-schein/.
9. Lisa Lerer, "Beyoncé, with Backup Dancers in Blue Pantsuits, Tries to Help Hillary in Ohio," *Boston Globe*, November 4, 2016, https://www.bostonglobe.com/news/politics/2016/11/04/clinton-campaign-taps-star-power-trump-goes-alone/n96t9SysJA0qcOCfnqvcoM/story.html.
10. Liz Bury, "Beyoncé Samples Chimamanda Ngozi Adichie's Call to Feminism," *The Guardian*, December 13, 2013, https://www.theguardian.com/books/2013/dec/13/beyonce-samples-chimamanda-ngozi-adichie-feminism-talk.
11. John Gross, "In France's Dreyfus Affair, the Artists, Too, Asked, 'Which Side Are You On?,'" *New York Times*, September 20, 1987, https://timesmachine.nytimes.com/timesmachine/1987/09/20/949487.html?pageNumber=333.
12. Philip McCouat, "Julie Manet, Renoir and the Dreyfus Affair," *Journal of Art in Society*, 2012 (updated 2021), https://www.artinsociety.com/julie-manet-renoir-and-the-dreyfus-affair.html.
13. Rachel Rodgers on Instagram, May 30, 2020, https://www.instagram.com/p/CA1Ez5qHL6o/?hl=en.
14. Simon Glickman, "In Tune with Lis Lewis," The Singers Workshop, 2022, https://thesingersworkshop.com/in-tune-with-lis-lewis/.
15. Robert Kelly, "'Sexy and Coy Without Trying Too Hard': How Britney Spears' 'Baby One More Time' Vocals Influenced a Generation," *Billboard*, October 25, 2018, https://www.billboard.com/articles/columns/pop/8481607/britney-spears-singing-voice-baby-one-more-time-vocals.
16. "Fix These 5 Money Mindset Blocks with Kelly Hollingsworth," *The Inspiration Place* (podcast), episode 92, June 2, 2020, https://www.schulmanart.com/2020/06/092-fix-these-5-money-mindset-blocks-with-kelly-hollingsworth/.

CHAPTER 7

1. Karen Weise and Michael Corkery, "People Now Spend More at Amazon Than at Walmart," *New York Times*, August 17, 2021, https://www.nytimes.com/2021/08/17/technology/amazon-walmart.html.
2. Jessi Devenyns, "Brand Loyalty Is Eroding Under Supply Chain and Price Pressures, Survey Finds," Grocery Dive, September 14, 2021, https://www.grocerydive.com/news/brand-loyalty-is-eroding-under-supply-chain-and-price-pressures-survey-fin/606757/.
3. Madeline Puckette, "Is Expensive Wine Worth It?" Wine Folly, n.d., https://winefolly.com/tips/is-expensive-wine-worth-it/.
4. Amanda Macmillan, "Why Wine Tastes Better When It Costs More," *Time*, August 16, 2017, https://time.com/4902359/wine-tastes-better-when-it-costs-more/.
5. Dan S. Kennedy and Jason Marrs, *No B.S. Price Strategy: The Ultimate No Holds Barred Kick Butt Take No Prisoner Guide to Profits, Power, and Prosperity* (Entrepreneur Press, 2011).
6. "Kick the Starving Artist Mentality with Money Mindset Mentor Denise Duffield-Thomas," *The Inspiration Place* (podcast), episode 33, April 2, 2019, https://www.schulmanart.com/2019/04/033-kick-the-starving-artist-mentality-with-money-mindset-mentor-denise-duffield-thomas/.
7. Cora Harrington, "About The Lingerie Addict," *The Lingerie Addict*, April 1, 2008, https://www.thelingerieaddict.com/2008/04/about-addict.html.
8. "State of the Consumer 2022," Win BIG Media, https://www.winbigmedia.com/state-of-consumers-2022.
9. Details come from Nathan Cole's website and also that of Jennifer Rosenfeld, his business coach.
10. See testimonial on https://jenniferrosenfeld.com/.
11. Graham Charlton, "The Importance of Customer Service for Loyalty and Retention," Sale Cycle, January 11, 2021, https://www.salecycle.com/blog/strategies/the-importance-of-customer-service-for-loyalty-and-retention/.
12. Linda Doucette shared this in a private coaching session. Permission has been granted to include her story in this book.
13. Stephie Grob Plante, "Shopping Has Become a Political Act. Here's How It Happened," Vox, October 7, 2019, https://www.vox.com/the-goods/2019/10/7/20894134/consumer-activism-conscious-consumerism-explained.
14. "State of the Consumer 2022."
15. Pamela N. Danziger, "Luxury Brands Need More Than Diversity to Prevent More Culturally Insensitive Mistakes," *Forbes*, March 3, 2019, https://www.forbes.com/sites/pamdanziger/2019/03/03/dolce-and-gabbana-gucci-burberry-caught-being-culturally-insensitive-diversity-isnt-the-fix/.

16. Maggie Zhang, "11 Psychological Tricks Restaurants Use to Make You Spend More Money," *Business Insider*, July 14, 2014, https://www .businessinsider.com.au/restaurant-menus-spend-more-money -2014-7.

17. Sybil S. Yang, Sheryl E. Kimes, and Mauro M. Sessarego, "$ or Dollars: Effects of Menu-Price Formats on Restaurant Checks," Cornell School of Hotel Administration, May 1, 2009, https://ecommons.cornell.edu /handle/1813/71169.

18. Monica Wadhwa and Kuangjie Zhang, "This Number Just Feels Right: The Impact of Roundedness of Price Numbers on Product Evaluations," *Journal of Consumer Research*, 41, no. 5 (February 2015), pp. 1172–1185, https://doi.org/10.1086/678484.

19. "How to Price Your Art with Jeffrey Shaw," *The Inspiration Place* (podcast), episode 3, August 28, 2018, https://www.schulmanart.com /2018/08/003-how-to-price-your-art-with-jeffrey-shaw/.

20. Naomi Pike, "As L'Oréal Paris' Famed Tagline 'Because You're Worth It' Turns 50, the Message Proves as Poignant as Ever," *Vogue*, March 8, 2021, https://www.vogue.co.uk/beauty/article/loreal-paris-because -youre worth it.

21. https://www.statista.com/statistics/243955/market-share-of-loreal -by-region/.

CHAPTER 8

1. Jack Flam, *Matisse in the Cone Collection: The Poetics of Vision* (Distributed by Penn State University Press for The Baltimore Museum of Art, 2001).

2. *A Modern Influence: Henri Matisse, Etta Cone, and Baltimore*, catalogue (Baltimore Museum of Art, 2021), https://artbma.org/exhibition/a-modern -influence-henri-matisse-etta-cone-and-baltimore/catalogue.

3. Miriam Schulman, "The Money Is in the List," *Professional Artist*, February/March 2018.

4. Miriam Schulman, "The Money Is in the List."

5. Miriam Schulman, "The Money Is in the List."

6. Miriam Schulman, "The Money Is in the List."

7. "Kosher," Urban Dictionary, https://www.urbandictionary.com/define .php?term=kosher.

8. "Ryan Deiss on the End of Marketing as We Know It (And I Feel Fine)," Digital Marketer, February 26, 2019, https://www.digitalmarketer.com /blog/end-of-marketing-as-we-know-it/.

9. Blair Feehan, "2022 Social Media Industry Benchmark Report," Rival IQ, February 15, 2022, https://www.rivaliq.com/blog/social-media -industry-benchmark-report/.

10. Johan Moreno, "TikTok Surpasses Google, Facebook as World's Most Popular Web Domain," *Forbes*, December 29, 2012, https://www.forbes

.com/sites/johanmoreno/2021/12/29/tiktok-surpasses-google
-facebook-as-worlds-most-popular-web-destination/.

11. Becky Hughes, "Food Businesses Lose Faith in Instagram After Algorithm Changes," *New York Times*, March 22, 2022, https://www.nytimes .com/2022/03/22/dining/instagram-algorithm-reels.html.

12. John Herrman, "Is There a Secret to Success on Instagram?" *New York Times*, January 26, 2021, https://www.nytimes.com/2021/01/26/style /instagram-growth-hack.html.

13. "Social Media Success Recipes with Italina Kirknis and Miriam Schulman," *The Inspiration Place* (podcast), episode 158, September 14, 2021, https://www.schulmanart.com/2021/09/158-social-media -success-recipes-with-italina-kirknis-and-miriam-schulman/.

14. Ben Smith, "Why We're Freaking Out About Substack," *New York Times*, April 11, 2021, https://www.nytimes.com/2021/04/11/business/media /substack-newsletter-competition.html.

15. "Don't Stay Quiet with Amy Porterfield," *The Inspiration Place* (podcast), episode 88, May 5, 2020, https://www.schulmanart.com/2020/05/088 -dont-stay-quiet-with-amy-porterfield/.

16. "Don't Stay Quiet with Amy Porterfield," *The Inspiration Place* (podcast), episode 88.

CHAPTER 9

1. A. H. Maslow, "A Theory of Human Motivation," *Psychological Review* 50, no. 4 (1943), pp. 370–396.

2. Janet Sikirica website, www.janetsikiricafiberarts.com.

3. "Inside Ballet Superstar Misty Copeland's Elegant New York City Home," *Architectural Digest*, YouTube video, uploaded September 1, 2020, https://www.youtube.com/watch?v=IxlzRwNX63A.

4. "Veblen Good," Investopedia, updated November 30, 2020, https:// www.investopedia.com/terms/v/veblen-good.asp.

5. Vanessa Friedman, "Michelle Obama Urged Everyone to Vote. Her Necklace Spelled It Out," *New York Times*, August 18, 2020, https://www .nytimes.com/2020/08/18/style/michelle-obama-necklace-DNC.html.

6. Alyssa Gregory, "7 Creative Ways to Use Emotions in Marketing," SitePoint, December 18, 2010, https://www.sitepoint.com/how-to-use -emotional-marketing/.

CHAPTER 10

1. Quotation taken from group coaching videoconference call inside the Artist Incubator coaching program on July 15, 2021.

2. "Stories That Stick with Kindra Hall and Miriam Schulman," *The Inspiration Place* (podcast), episode 151, July 27, 2021, https://www

.schulmanart.com/2021/07/151-stories-that-stick-with-kindra-hall-and
-miriam-schulman/.

3. "How to Sell Your Art Class (No Flowery Words Required) with Danielle Weil," *The Inspiration Place* (podcast), episode 105, September 1, 2020, https://www.schulmanart.com/2020/09/105-how-to-sell-your-art -class-no-flowery-words-required-with-danielle-weil/

CHAPTER 11

1. Richard Wiseman, "New Year's Resolution Project," n.d., http://www .richardwiseman.com/quirkology/new/USA/Experiment_resolution .shtml.
2. Peter Economy, "This Is the Way You Need to Write Down Your Goals for Faster Success," *Inc.*, February 28, 2018, https://www.inc.com/peter -economy/this-is-way-you-need-to-write-down-your-goals-for -faster-success.html.
3. "How Does Writing Affect Your Brain?" NeuroRelay, August 7, 2013, https://neurorelay.com/2013/08/07/how-does-writing-affect-your -brain/.
4. Sarah Gardner and Dave Albee, "Study Focuses on Strategies for Achieving Goals, Resolutions," press release, Dominican University of California, February 1, 2015, https://scholar.dominican.edu/cgi /viewcontent.cgi?article=1265&context=news-releases.
5. Stacey Colino, "Decision Fatigue: Why It's So Hard to Make Up Your Mind These Days, and How to Make It Easier," *Seattle Times*, September 23, 2021, https://www.seattletimes.com/nation-world/decision-fatigue -why-its-so-hard-to-make-up-your-mind-these-days-and-how-to -make-it-easier/.
6. Maria Konnikova, "Multitask Masters," *New Yorker*, May 7, 2014, https:// www.newyorker.com/science/maria-konnikova/multitask-masters.
7. John Medina, *Brain Rules: 12 Principles for Surviving and Thriving at Work, Home, and School* (Pear Press, 2008).
8. May Wong, "Stanford Study Finds Walking Improves Creativity," Stanford report, April 24, 2014, https://news.stanford.edu/news/2014 /april/walking-vs-sitting-042414.html.
9. David Surrenda, "The Purpose of Yoga," *New York Times*, January 12, 2012, https://www.nytimes.com/roomfordebate/2012/01/12/is-yoga -for-narcissists/the-purpose-of-yoga.
10. "Authentic Expression and Passionate Bliss with Dr. Valerie Rein," *The Inspiration Place* (podcast), episode 124, January 19, 2021, https://www .schulmanart.com/2021/01/124-authentic-expression-and-passionate -bliss-with-dr-valerie-rein/.
11. Rick Hanson, PhD, and Rick Mendius, MD, "Buddha's Brain: The New Neuroscience and the Path of Awakening," https://www.rickhanson

.net/buddhas-brain-the-new-neuroscience-and-the-path-of
-awakening-inquiring-mind/.

12. "How to Get Your Art Noticed with Elizabeth Mordensky and Miriam Schulman," *The Inspiration Place* (podcast), episode 164, October 26, 2021, https://www.schulmanart.com/2021/10/164-how-to-get-your-art -noticed-with-elizabeth-mordensky-and-miriam-schulman/.

13. "Hire Your First VA with Jen Lehner," *The Inspiration Place* (podcast), episode 75, February 4, 2020, https://www.schulmanart.com/2020/02 /075-hire-your-first-va-with-jen-lehner/.

14. "The Alter Ego Effect with Peak Performance Coach Todd Herman," *The Inspiration Place* (podcast), episode 43, June 25, 2019, https://www .schulmanart.com/2019/06/043-the-alter-ego-effect-with-peak -performance-coach-todd-herman/.

15. Madhav Goyal, Sonal Singh, Erica M. S. Sibinga, et al, "Meditation Programs for Psychological Stress and Well-Being: A Systematic Review and Meta-analysis," *JAMA Intern Med.* 174, no. 3 (2014), pp. 357– 368, https://jamanetwork.com/journals/jamainternalmedicine /fullarticle/1809754.

16. Simon Baijot, Hichet Slama, Göran Söderlund, Bernard Dan, Paul Deltenre, Cécile Colin, and Nicolas Deconink, "Neuropsychological and Neurophysiological Benefits from White Noise in Children with and without ADHD," *Behav Brain Funct* 12, no. 11 (2016), https://doi.org/10.1186 /s12993-016-0095-y.

17. David Allen, *Getting Things Done: The Art of Stress-Free Productivity*, revised edition (Penguin Books, 2015).

CHAPTER 12

1. "Get Inspired by Global Pop Artist Ashley Longshore," The Inspiration Place, August 21, 2018, https://www.schulmanart.com/2018/08/001-get -inspired-by-global-pop-artist-ashley-longshore/.

2. Ian Cook, "Who Is Driving the Great Resignation?" *Harvard Business Review*, September 15, 2021, https://hbr.org/2021/09/who-is-driving-the -great-resignation.

3. This is a little Easter egg I planted for those who are familiar with *Waiting for Godot*. Throughout the play, Estragon agonizes about his boots, taking them on and off, symbolizing our daily struggles. These are the circumstances in life, but what will make all the difference is not to blame your boots, or rather your circumstances, and to keep moving forward.

INDEX

+ + + + + + + +